REWARDING AND RECOGNIZING EMPLOYEES

Ideas for Individuals, Teams, and Managers

The Briefcase Books Series

Managing Stress: Keeping Calm Under Fire
Barbara I Braham

Business Negotiating Basics
Peter Economy

Straight Answers to People Problems
Fred E. Jandt

Empowering Employees Through Delegation
Robert B. Nelson

Better Business Meetings
Robert B. Nelson
Peter Economy

The Presentation Primer: Getting Your Point Across
Robert B. Nelson
Jennifer Wallick

Listen for Success: A Guide to Effective Listening
Arthur K. Robertson

The New Manager's Handbook
Brad Thompson

REWARDING AND RECOGNIZING EMPLOYEES
Ideas for Individuals, Teams, and Managers

Joan P. Klubnik

McGraw-Hill
New York   San Francisco   Washington, D.C.   Auckland   Bogotá
Caracas   Lisbon   London   Madrid   Mexico City   Milan
Montreal   New Delhi   San Juan   Singapore
Sydney   Tokyo   Toronto

McGraw-Hill

A Division of The McGraw-Hill Companies

Library of Congress Cataloging-in-Publication Data

Klubnik, Joan P.
   Rewarding and recognizing employees: ideas for individuals, teams, and managers / Joan P. Klubnik.
      p. cm.—(Briefcase books series)
   Includes index.
   ISBN 0-7863-0297-6.—ISBN 0-7863-0349-2 (international ed.)
   1. Incentives in industry.   2. Employee motivation.   I. Title.
II. Series.
HF5549.5.I5K53   1995
658.3\14—dc20   94–36127

Printed in the United States of America
   6 7 8 9 10 QPV 02 01 00 99

The Briefcase Books Series

Research shows that people who buy business books (1) want books that can be read quickly, perhaps on a plane trip, commuting on a train, or overnight, and (2) feel their time and money were well spent if they get two or three useful insights or techniques for improving their professional skills or helping them with a current problem at work.

Briefcase Books were designed to meet these two criteria. They focus on necessary skills and problem areas, and include real-world examples from practicing managers and professionals. Inside these books you'll find useful, practical information and techniques in a straightforward, concise, and easy-to-read format.

This book and others like it in the Briefcase Books series can quickly give you insights and answers regarding your current needs and problems. And they are useful references for future situations and problems.

If you find this book or any other in this series to be of value, please share it with your co-workers. With tens of thousands of new books published each year, any book that can simplify the growing complexities in managing others needs to be circulated as widely as possible.

Robert B. Nelson
Series Editor

Foreword

My mission in life has been to be a conveyor of simple truths. It is for that reason that I'm pleased to be able to introduce the Briefcase Books series, which seeks to provide simple, practical, and direct answers to the most common problems managers face on a daily basis.

It has been my experience that in the field of business, common sense is not common practice. So it is refreshing to find a series of books that glorifies common sense in dealing with people in the workplace.

Take the skill of listening. We all know that it is important to listen, yet how many of us actually do it well? I suggest it would be rare to find one in a hundred managers that is truly a good listener. Most people focus on what they are going to say next when someone else is talking. They would seldom if ever think to check what they thought they heard to make sure it is accurate. And they seldom acknowledge or attempt to deal with emotions when they occur in speaking with someone at work. These are basic errors in the use of this basic skill. And regardless of how much education or experience you have, you should know how to listen.

But how much training have you had on the topic of listening? Have you ever had a course on the topic? Have you ever tested your ability to listen? Have you ever discussed with others how you could listen better with greater comprehension and respect? Probably not. Even though this fundamental interpersonal skill could cripple the most talented individual if he or she is not good at it.

Fortunately, listening is just one of the fundamental skills singled out for its own volume in the Briefcase Books series. Others include books on making presentations, negotiating, problem solving, and handling stress. And other volumes are planned even as I write this.

The Briefcase Books series focuses on those basic skills that managers must master to excel at work. Whether you are new to managing or are a seasoned manager, you'll find these books of value in obtaining useful insights and fundamental knowledge you can use for your entire career.

Ken Blanchard
Co-author
The One Minute Manager

Preface

This book helps you, the individual contributor, the team unit, or the organization to better understand the many facets of rewarding and recognizing employees. The book includes a look at:

- The attitudes and skills of individual contributors that ultimately determine whether a person values and practices the reward and recognition process.
- The strategic, big-picture role of recognition in the organization, which determines whether recognition is a process or program within the organization.

Today's changing environment, with its greater emphasis upon teams and individual contributors, increases the importance of broad-based reward and recognition systems. Through the use of the various self-assessment, planning exercises, and examples of recognition in action, you will be encouraged to assess your own effectiveness as a giver (and receiver) of recognition. You also will be able to determine what you want for your team and for your organization, and you will learn ways to help you achieve this desired state—with a degree of levity.

Rewards and recognition are basic tenets of quality. As with all facets of a quality initiative, you need to think of recognition in terms of its being a *journey* and part of a commitment to continuous improvement. Simply putting a recognition program in place will not make rewards and recognition an integral part of your organization, nor will it automatically result in improved employee morale and motivation—which are at the heart of increased productivity and job satisfaction. The value of this book is that it can help you to take advantage of the power of recognition as a tool for personal and organizational competitive advantage.

Regardless of your organization's position, you are free to incorporate recognition within *your sphere* of influence. Accept ownership for seeing that recognition is personally practiced by you. This personal ownership is the heart of a successful rewards and recognition system.

The chapters of this book will lead you from a personal focus through to a corporate model for rewarding and recognizing the contributions made by individuals within the organization. Think in terms of a puzzle.

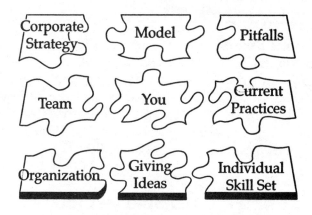

Each piece of the puzzle is important, but the picture will be discernible even if some pieces are missing (i.e., recognition can be practiced even when a piece is missing). Obviously, the fewer missing pieces and the more interlocked the pieces are, the more complete your rewards and recognition picture will be. What you learn about each puzzle piece by reading this book will help you enhance your entire recognition process.

CHAPTER 1: ATTITUDES ABOUT RECOGNITION

Recognition is ultimately a personal action. This chapter focuses on personal attitudes about recognition: how an individual's thinking and behavior around rewards and recognition will impact the type and degree of recognition that the individual participates in. In addition, the attitudes of teams and the organization are also reviewed. Is recognition treated as a program, or as a *process*? The value of recognition to daily operations is addressed.

CHAPTER 2: RECOGNITION AS A LEADERSHIP STRATEGY

This chapter focuses on how recognition fits in with corporate vision, long-term strategies, and tactical operational planning. Information about why recognition should be considered strategic is included, as are tips on how to make this happen. You can use the information in this chapter to begin to assess and enhance the strategic positioning of recognition in your organization.

CHAPTER 3: MEASURING CURRENT RECOGNITION PATTERNS

This chapter helps you assess and profile recognition you currently have in place. Both individual and corporate patterns are looked at. You will develop a personal picture of the gaps between what you have in place and what you would like. Ways to address typical recognition gaps are explored.

CHAPTER 4: THE RECOGNITION PROCESS—SKILLS NEEDED TO MAKE IT HAPPEN

Effective recognition relies upon a set of skills that individuals do not always apply. This chapter provides a "what-is-needed" map for rewards and recognition to work within teams and within the organization at large. Skills needed for both management-driven and peer-to-peer processes are described and techniques for their development are reviewed.

CHAPTER 5: ESTABLISHING A MODEL PROGRAM

This chapter presents an implementation plan that leaders can follow to establish recognition within teams and organizations. Both management-driven and peer-to-peer forms of recognition are addressed.

CHAPTER 6: PITFALLS TO WATCH OUT FOR

This chapter points out typical obstacles that surface, ones that can prevent recognition from being as effective as it might be in an organization. Obstacles that occur because of program design, corporate culture issues, and human attitudes in both managers and employees are addressed. The pitfalls are presented along with potential solutions.

CHAPTER 7: RECOGNITION IDEAS

This chapter provides a variety of recognition ideas. Categories include corporate-controlled recognition as well as no-cost/low-cost ideas appropriate for teams and individual peer giving.

Note: Included throughout the book are a variety of examples drawn from recognition experiences and processes that have been shared by many individuals. A conscious decision was made to not attribute specific examples to specific organizations. For this reason the examples have been written in generic/non-organization-specific format.

As you apply the recognition skills and ideas presented in this book, I would like to hear of your successes and challenges (my phone number is 714–965–6770 or my fax number is 714–964–1011). Together, we can continue to enhance the recognition process in the business community.

Joan P. Klubnik

Contents

Chapter Seven
RECOGNITION IDEAS   130

Chapter One

Attitudes about Recognition

In today's corporations, which are becoming more team- and individual-contributor focused, individuals can benefit by understanding how their attitudes about the recognition process relate to their willingness to get involved. Employees' attitudes can range from:

Disempowered—an attitude that puts recognition in the hands of the corporation. Statements individuals might make that reflect this mind set include: "Management and the company `own' recognition; the managers are responsible for recognizing employee contributions. I can't really do anything to recognize others unless the company sanctions it."

To *Empowered*—The individual is responsible for her own sphere of influence. Statements reflecting this mind set toward recognition might include: "I'm in charge of seeing that I notice and recognize the contributions of those around me. It doesn't matter what my job is, I'm responsible for the recognition I give to others. I'll recognize a peer regardless of what my manager does or doesn't do to show appreciation."

Your past experiences with the recognition process will affect your ability to reward and to recognize others. This is true regardless of your position in the organization. When you consider today's workplace—doing more with

Figure 1-1
Recognition Impact Spiral

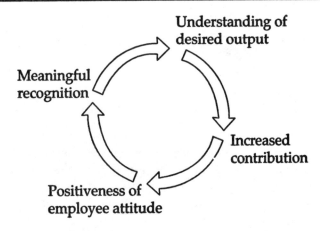

less, workforce reductions, high levels of workplace stress, the uncertainties generated by work process redesign and reengineering—the appeal of recognition as a way to counter these forces is strong. One of the key values of recognition within a corporation is its ability to act as a motivator and reinforcer of desirable behavior. It can influence the way employees feel about themselves and their contributions to the organization's output. These in turn influence job satisfaction and thus productivity.

The interaction among recognition, productivity, and individual employee attitude is shown in Figure 1-1. This figure represents a spiral that can move in one of two directions. Moving upward, it elevates each element to a higher plane—the essence of continuous improvement. Moving downward, it results in a dysfunctional work group. Although recognition is only one element in the cycle, it is a powerful drive of the spiral's direction.

Figure 1–2
Continuum of Attitude about Giving Recognition

Total Self-Centeredness	I feel good	I believe in the	Total Other-Centeredness
What I can personally get by giving recognition to someone else (i.e., how I can manipulate to my best interest).	giving recognition, and I know the person appreciates what I'm giving and the way in which I'm giving it.	value of recognition totally, but I am not particularly comfortable giving it. However, I'll do it if it will make others happy or motivated and more productive.	How I feel about recognition is totally unimportant. Only the person receiving the reward counts, so I'll do whatever I must no matter how it makes me feel

∧

The effectiveness of recognition is impacted by the attitude of the person giving it. As shown in Figure 1–2, attitudes about recognition can be thought of as gradations between the extremes of self-centeredness and other-centeredness.

Where do you place yourself on the continuum? The extremes are counterproductive. When people operate from either of these two extreme mind sets, the recognition given will reflect the dysfunctional attitudes driving it. Recognition at its best and most effective represents something we do for others while accommodating our own style and needs. It is found in the middle of the continuum. As a process, it should make us feel glad that we did what we did and should account for the other person's reaction to the act. When this occurs, recognition is a win/win process.

The giver's attitude about the process is important because it influences the nonverbal messages that accompany the recognition. The best recognition is given by individuals who consider rewards to be a win/win prospect—where both the giver and the receiver gain as a result of the process. Without this mind-set, recognition giving will probably be less than successful. The giver will be frustrated, because she thought she was doing the right thing, and the receiver will be dissatisfied because of the nonverbal messages encountered during the giving process. Ninety-three percent of your message is carried by nonverbals, and these signals override the words that you prepare. Your body is the prime reflector of the way you actually think and feel about the recognition process. The recipient will pick up on the clues that you give, whether consciously or subconsciously.

What is your attitude about recognition? Take a minute to complete the exercise in the accompanying box.

Think about recognition you've experienced in the past, both as a giver and as a receiver. List the first 10 words that come to your mind regarding recognition and how you feel about your experiences with the process.

_____   _____

_____   _____

_____   _____

_____   _____

_____   _____

Now reread your list, putting a plus before all the positive words and a minus before the negative words. Leave blank those that you consider to be neutral. Total your number of positive, negative, and neutral responses:

Total number of positive words: _____	Total number of negative words: _____	Total number of neutral words: _____

How do your numbers look? Obviously you want more positive than negative words. Do you think the attitudes you reflected above through your choice of words affect any recognition that you give? The answer is yes because of the nonverbals that always accompany human activity.

Think about your past behavior in situations when you were the giver of recognition. Did you:

- Like the experience? (You were comfortable in what you were saying, what you were giving, and in the reaction of the recipient.)

- Feel it was okay? (You don't do it that often, so you weren't really sure of what to say. The other person seemed to like what recognition you gave, but he didn't seem to be any more comfortable than you with the entire process.)

- Hate it? (You avoid directly giving any recognition whenever possible. Written thank-you's and recommendations for formal recognition are OK, but you don't like doing it in person.)

Acknowledge your own feelings. If you tend toward the *hate it* side, it is especially important that you recognize this and then think about why you feel as you do. There is a relationship between how you feel about giving recognition and the frequency with which you give it. Feeling good about recognition equates with more giving.

So, is there anything you can do if you don't feel comfortable with the process? Yes, the good news is that the giving process is a learned skill. You can become more proficient even if you don't especially like doing it. You'll learn about recognition-giving skills in Chapter 4. These skills include:

- Reading nonverbals, both yours and those in others.
- Voicing observations about others' contributions.
- Watching and listening to see what is being done by others.
- Learning "thank-you scripts" and using them.

However, before you begin to develop these skills, you will need to recognize your feelings about the process. This allows you to develop your own recognition templates. Ones with which you can be comfortable and that accommodate your attitudes. Regardless of your feelings and comfort with giving recognition, you can develop effective giving techniques. Part of the effectiveness stems from selecting behaviors that complement your comfort level. This results in a more natural posture for the giving.

Example: You are uncomfortable with large groups and public situations, so you learn to give recognition one-on-one. Or, if recognition must be public, you rely on structured giving that lets someone else do the talking in public.

If you are not comfortable with the recognition process, take a few minutes to answer each of the questions below in the space provided:

- Why is it that you don't give recognition very often?

  _____ _____

  _____ _____

  _____ _____

  _____

- On whom do you focus when you give recognition—
  yourself and your own feelings or the recipient and
  his feelings? _____ _____

  _____ _____

  _____ _____

  _____

  _____

- What would it take to make you more comfortable
  with the process—ways it could be done, people
  involved, vehicles used? Be specific. _____

  _____ _____

  _____

  _____

  _____

- Whom in your organization are you most comfortable
  recognizing? Think of specific people and name
  names. _____ _____

  _____

  _____ _____

  _____

  _____ _____

- Is there anyone you respect who regularly recognizes others? How does she do it? Are there things she does that you could emulate or borrow? _____

  _____

  _____

  _____

- What are the payoffs that reinforce your not giving more recognition than you do—no company incentive to do so, easier to not give than to give, it's never hurt your career not to give recognition? _____

  _____

  _____

  _____

- What advantages might there be in you giving more recognition than you do? _____

  _____

  _____

  _____

  _____

Answering these questions about attitudes and behaviors will help you formulate a plan for increasing your comfort with giving because they identify specific action-planning areas that can improve the quality of what is given and the skills of you, the giver. If you want to begin making changes in your recognition-giving behavior, go back through your responses to the preceding statements and use the information to create a written action statement that you are willing to commit to. Incorporate those points that you feel affect your giving. Following through on your written action statement will improve your ability to recognize the contributions of others

INFLUENCE OF THE TEAM AND THE CORPORATION ON ATTITUDES

Each of us brings to the workplace our personal attitudes toward recognition—how we feel about giving it, getting it, and our need for it. These attitudes obviously affect how we deal with recognition on the job. In addition, there are two other major influencers: the attitudes toward giving recognition demonstrated by the team and those demonstrated by the company at large. Each team or organization has its own culture, or norms, which influences and tempers recognition-giving behavior regardless of an individual's personal, private attitudes about rewards. If you work on a team or in an organization that prizes recognition, you will be much more likely to give it to others, to be aware of situations which warrant it, and to be gracious when you are receiving it. On the other hand, if your team or organization does not favor giving recognition, you will limit the amount you give or find circuitous ways of doing so to avoid countering the norms.

Today, corporate influence is important. Tomorrow, a major source of influence will be the emerging self-directed team. This unit, when successful, will be staffed by people who are empowered to take action. One request voiced by today's teams is for information about effective ways to acknowledge and recognize each other's performance. In the new environment, the old norm of recognition that is minimal and controlled by management will no longer be acceptable. Managers who believe in and model the old style will need to change to succeed in the new team-based and peer-driven paradigm. There will be a migration from corporate influence over recognition patterns to individuals and teams holding influence over these processes.

In one organization the norm had been for all discretionary bonuses to be controlled by management. As teams developed and took on more responsibility, the rules were changed so that today each team is able to access its cost-center's bonus dollars. Some boundaries were set by the company—maximum amount for an individual bonus and how much money was set aside for the fiscal year. Beyond this, the teams control their own allocation, including the right to give bonuses to people outside the team itself.

The ingrained management attitudes driving some of today's recognition-giving styles will not change easily. Having the new team norms for recognition incorporated into the performance management system will motivate individuals to change. Tying recognition behavior to performance appraisal will be key to large scale change within any organization.

What are your team's and your corporation's attitudes about recognition? Some awareness of a company's attitudes toward recognition can be gained by answering each of the following questions:

1. When you walk through the work area, do you see lots of visible proof of recognition—objects like banners, pictures, and bulletin boards recognizing contributions? **Yes No**

2. Are people able to play (congratulatory parties, posters, and mementos are visible evidence that people take recognition playfully)? **Yes No**

3. If you stopped someone, could the person relate a "story" about receiving, giving, or personally observing recognition in action? **Yes No**

4. Is it evident that recognition belongs to   **Yes   No**
   everyone, that it is not just a formal program managed by human resources?

5. Are people evaluated in part on the   **Yes   No**
   amount of recognition they give to others?

6. Are there tools and vehicles in place that   **Yes   No**
   allow people to reward others?

Look over your answers to the above questions. "Yes" answers reflect behaviors that support positive corporate attitudes toward recognition. They also provide a basis for strategies and represent specific skills or actions that can be woven into daily business operations to further a recognition-driven culture. "No" answers reflect a culture that does not value recognition (i.e., that doesn't see the value-added contribution made by recognition and thus does not encourage the introduction of a recognition *process*).

To understand your own team or organization, begin at the top. How often do senior managers get involved, initiating recognition or participating in informal processes? Unless key people (your senior management team) are involved, you cannot expect recognition processes to flourish. If you deal with such a group at the top, you will need to develop a marketing strategy to sell the value-added contribution of recognition to that team.

Demonstrating the dollar benefits of a recognition program to an organization can assist you with selling it. To make it a *process* will take longer and require more work than will introducing a "token" program. This is because a process requires *walking the talk* on the part of the management team. This happens when they believe in and live recognition. Some specific actions you can take to accomplish the selling process in your organization include the following:

• Repeat your message of cost/benefit on a regular basis—reinforce the value to the organization of senior management supporting recognition. Create a report that shows what has been done in a given period of time and convert this to show the dollar benefits for the organization.

• Share success and war stories, especially ones that involve senior managers doing things that support recognition. Be sure you incorporate measurement.

Example: In one organization, the president created "presidential dollars," which he empowered all employees to give as the "coin of the realm." The purpose was to recognize cost-saving actions. Employees involved in a project estimated how much it could save the company. The estimate was exchanged for dollars. The estimates provided a measure of the actual amount of savings employees were generating. Employees had "tokens" that could be exchanged for perquisites.

• Make it easy for your target audience to give the kind of recognition you want given within the organization so they will be more willing to give it a try.

An organization that wanted to have its workforce hear about recognition has included a column in the company newspaper devoted to stories about people who went out of their way to recognize the contributions of others. The story always focuses on the person giving the recognition (what kind of "giving" was done) rather than on the contribution being recognized—thus providing a model for the desired behavior. Over time it has become an honor to be written up in the paper.

Changing behavior (attitudes too) takes time. Research in self-development has shown that new behaviors take approximately 20 tries before they are assimilated into a person's repertoire. Plan ahead before you ask senior people to do more recognition or before you attempt to include more

As part of the company's move to a team environment, a climate survey was completed. After analysis, it was decided that senior management needed to do more "walk ing around" and to become more actively involved with employees—especially in the area of giving recognition.

The president was not particularly comfortable interacting with employees—commenting on work in progress, saying thank you personally to an outstanding employee—so a strategy was developed to help him have more direct involvement. Initial efforts were focused on the accounting department because that was the discipline he was most comfortable with. Whenever he went into the work area to walk around and thank an employe, at least one key person from the area accompanied him to make introductions, guide small talk, and provide support. With this beginning the president was well received and became more comfortable with the process. Eventually, he reached a point at which he would spontaneously go out without support.

team-based and spontaneous, peer-to-peer giving in the organization. Understand that it will be a time consuming project. Consider the following:

- The higher up the corporate ladder, the less open an individual is to trying out new things.
- The less your team or organization values recognition based on its demonstrated behavior of giving, the harder it will be for key people to embrace a new attitude.

If you wish to institute a new recognition process, you must be ready to support early attempts on the part of your target audience to try out the new behaviors—this is true regardless of the audience you have targeted. Early success will influence how willing people will be to try out additional recognition behaviors. Look to create safe environments for them to begin trying these new behaviors. The more homework you have done to ready recipients (including picking the right people for initial involvement), the better your chances are to get the 20 tries that behavior modification and attitude change require.

How committed are you to developing the "right attitudes" about recognition on your team or in your organization? Honestly address whether you are willing to tackle the job of changing how people think about recognition in the organization. If you aren't willing to tackle it at this point, focus on how you can personally support the concept. Commit to readdressing the appropriateness of recognition for the team or organization at a specific point in the future.

If you aren't ready today to address the appropriateness of recognition for your organization or team, when will you be ready to do so?

_____
        (specific date)

Be prepared. Some people view a "plan" to change attitudes and behavior as devious and manipulative. You can counter such thoughts by focusing on how recognition provides value-added to the team or corporation. Think: Who will benefit? How will the organization, team, or individual contributor be better for the change? Developing interventions to change the attitude or behavior of individuals is time-consuming and is proportional to the size of the audience. Consider up front how committed you are to the effort. Unless commitment is high, don't embark on the journey.

If you choose to proceed, identify some form of recognition that will benefit your team or organization and plan

Recognition has always been "serious stuff." The new CEO wanted more recognition of individual contribution, so she instituted an ADDA BUCK program. Everyone was given $25 worth of "bucks" that could be given to co-workers whenever one wished to recognize the efforts of another. The bucks could be accumulated for merchandise offered through the company catalog. Interestingly, most people preferred to post their bucks in their work space so that others could see visible proof of the amount of recognition an individual had received. It was quite common to hear squeals of delight as bucks exchanged hands.

A new tone was set during the six months the program was in effect, and most people became more aware of the contribution of co-workers. This served as a preparatory step toward developing self-directed team skills—the ability to respect and acknowledge team member contribution.

for situations that will encourage the appropriate behavior and attitude. The goal is to create an environment in which positive recognition-giving behavior is easy for the targeted individuals so they can experience it and learn about its benefits first hand—this is the heart of attitude change.

Efforts to change attitudes and behaviors can be furthered by an assessment of the skills required for effective recognition giving. This will be discussed in Chapter 4. If you can ensure that people have the opportunity to develop the skills needed to give recognition, you can influence their attitudes about it. In this chapter, you learned about the attitudes of the current state of your organization and its employees, the next step is to create or identify an organization recognition strategy. Chapter 2 will help you focus on where you want the organization to be regarding rewards and recognition and will help you establish your leadership role in the migration process.

Chapter 2

Recognition as a Leadership Strategy

Reward   1: Something that is given in return for good . . . done or received and especially that is offered or given for some service or attainment. 2: A stimulus administered . . . following a correct or desired response that increases the probability of occurrence of the response.

Recognition   1: Acknowledgment. 2: A special notice or attention.[1]

To be seen as a leader in your organization, you must learn to *reward* and *recognize* the efforts of those around you. Taking the initiative to say thank you is a relatively untapped leadership strategy. Yet recognition is probably one of the most powerful job motivators that we have available to us. Its simplicity, impact, and availability are almost boundless. Recognition is a powerful leadership tool because it is appropriate for everyone in the organization.

Everyone in an organization can and should be skilled at recognizing the efforts of others. The keys to recognition

---

[1]*Websters Ninth New Collegiate Dictionary* (Springfield, MA: Merriam-Webster, Inc., 1986).

effectiveness are in the honest passion and caring that drive it. These can be nurtured and enhanced by a management team who have taken the time to understand the value of developing a recognition strategy and who have taken the initiative to see that everyone in the organization has the necessary skills and tools.

Saying that recognition is important is like saying that motherhood and apple pie are something everyone believes in and supports. Yet, consider the following scenarios that are typical of comments offered by people within companies throughout the United States. These comments were made by people who work hard in organizations that *think* they recognize their employees effectively. However, these employee statements reveal that the employees feel their efforts are often not recognized or are inappropriately recognized.

You know, I stayed up most of the night and worked through the next day into the evening. And, do you know what? He didn't even say "Thank you" or even acknowledge all the extra effort I put in to see that his job ran correctly!

She really did a lot of extra work to help the team complete its project. The entire team wants to thank her by celebrating together, but we don't know what to do or say. We can't go overboard or it might set a precedent for other team projects. We don't know what would be appropriate. She must intuitively know she did a good job and that we appreciate her effort. Maybe we shouldn't do anything after all.

Last month I asked my manager to give Tish some kind of nonmonetary recognition for all the help given on that last project. So far nothing has happened. I just don't know how to get my manager to do anything. I wish there was some way I could be more proactive to see that efforts are recognized around here.

Do any of these sound familiar? Take a minute to think about yourself and your recognition-giving patterns. What does recognition mean to you in the context of your organization? Think about the last three times you recognized another employee in your organization. Describe in writing *who* was recognized, *what* the recognition was for, and *why* it was given. The writing process is important because it will force you to recall details. If you have difficulty with this exercise, consider why this is so. Is it because you rarely give recognition? Also, take a minute to look at your description. Are the people from different strata or areas of the organization? Were the events being recognized different? What about your motivator for giving—the WIIFM (What's In It For Me) for you and for the recipient?

Today's employees have an increased need for support systems to help reduce the stress caused by workplace redesign and reengineering. Successful organizations will learn to tap into rewards and recognition as a strategic resource. Rewards and recognition make good business sense and help people deal more effectively with a workplace in turmoil.

Most employees find casual dress days to be a reward of sorts. Many organizations are allowing reengineering teams to dress casually throughout the meeting process (this can be full time for a month or two or can be spread out over time with a day or two per week of meeting), unless there is a business reason to do otherwise.

Think about yourself. When were you last *effectively* recognized (i.e., you knew you had exerted extra or special effort, and you appreciated the reward that was given to you)? What did this recognition do to your feelings about your job and your efforts? Take a minute to remember the incident and then write a short description of the event and the impact it had on your behavior and thoughts.

What *you* remember and value in any recognition—its impact on you personally—is the heart of effective recognition. Successful reward strategies recognize and build upon the fact that not everyone wants to be recognized in the same way. A strategy needs to include recognition vehicles that are available to every employee and that account for those who prefer to be recognized by peers rather than by management. A frequent complaint about recognition is its formality and its distance from the receiver. A leadership strategy needs to be in place to counter the view of recognition as a management prerogative.

Managers and leaders who understand the power of recognition, its simplicity, its ease of implementation, and its positive influence will be the most successful because they will personally apply recognition and they will actively encourage others in the organization to do the same.

Effective managers appreciate the importance of recognition. You will often see these individuals wandering through the facility. They are quick to thank people personally for their contributions. If someone is receiving some sort of recognition, the manager will be there—not overshadowing the people who initiated the recognition, but to let people know she cares, too.

For example, a team put together a big banner that everyone signed, and someone brought in a decorated cupcake to give to the team member being honored. The manager was there, laughing with everyone else and signing the banner. Because this manager is always there, everyone is comfortable with his appearance and participation—he does not inhibit the process.

Recognition can impact an organization's effectiveness both positively and negatively. Companies that encourage employees to recognize each others' contributions are rewarded with a healthier environment in which staff members openly and comfortably interact with each other. When you acknowledge and praise the positive, people are much more open in their relationships—a key component of effective communication and a characteristic that most workers seek in a job.

Recognition can be a cornerstone to an open-communication environment because it reinforces desired behavior and it creates an atmosphere of appreciation and trust in which people are more likely to communicate openly. People focus more on each other's positive contributions because these are brought to their attention through the recognition process. This is a strategy that should involve everyone in the organization and is most effective when initiated at the top. Modeling by senior staff sets the tone for all employees as people watch and emulate the communication and recognition patterns of those in charge.

Take a minute to review your organization's communication patterns. How open are they? Are people encouraged to recognize each other's contributions? Do they provide input about all types of work-related behaviors, especially positive ones? Such communication must be consciously established and plans must be implemented to ensure that it is instituted and maintained. Think about your current communication environment. Be sure to write out your responses. Remember, clarity of thought and action come through the writing process.

- How free are people to comment on one another's contributions and behaviors? _____

_____

_____

- Would you consider your feedback process to be a plus in your organization's culture? _____

  _____

  _____

- Are you pleased with the current situation? Do your communication patterns encourage recognition? _____

  _____

  _____

- If you could make changes to improve communication and thus recognition, what would these be? _____

  _____

  _____

Recognition is a *pulling* strategy. Employees experience managers practicing recognition, like the way it feels, and are "pulled" into the process—first as recipients and then as initiators. However, managers can't say they believe in rewarding and recognizing people and then do nothing. As the quality process has taught and emphasized, management must *walk the talk*. Look back at your responses to the preceding items. Do they reflect a *pulling* effort? Is there evidence of a conscious plan to incorporate one?

A strategy is a high-level plan, one that focuses on the big-picture aspects of goal setting and accomplishment. If an organization is to use recognition as a pulling strategy, the following will need to be considered:

- Relationship to vision and goals—this reflects the philosophy of senior management and influences the organization's culture. Recognition, if truly a strategy, will be spelled out at some point in the visioning process (i.e., a part of the philosophy statement, an objective, a critical success factor).

- Clarity around how giving rewards and recognition benefits the organization—it must be positioned as value-added. Everyone must recognize that the time and effort spent on recognition results in payback to the organization.
- Clear implementation plans must be in place—this is the translation of strategy into a "living" business driver.
- There must be a champion of recognition at a high level within the organization—the reality in organizations is that things that are supported by key senior managers become a part of the environment. Someone at the senior level must believe in and actively and openly support recognition if it is to be a strategic tool.

The focus on strategy should not discount the efforts of teams and individual employees who consciously make the effort to reward and recognize others in the organization. However, a rewards and recognition system will be "officially" embraced and implemented only to the degree of support demonstrated by senior management.

What should you do when you can't get the management support you desire? **Assume control of your own sphere of influence.** Take the view that even though you can't influence what those above and around you do in the organization, you can behave and model the behavior you desire. Too often individuals simply give up: "What can I do? How can I alone make a difference? Why should I when my manager doesn't?" The preceding statements reflect a relinquishing of control. Each of us can take charge of our own behavior. If you believe in recognition, then be sure you demonstrate that belief through the kind and amount you bestow on others. Create your *own* vision and live it.

The company half-heartedly supported recognition—a formal program was in place but no nonmonetary opportunities were present. One manager had a vision for the training team: to see that everyone in the organization was exposed to the new word-processing standard. He gave the training team the "green light" to figure out how to do this and then to follow through on the ideas. The team met its goal and decided it needed to celebrate its accomplishment of training its 1,000th person within six months. They held a "green party" to build on the idea of the green light the manager had given. Everyone brought green food—green punch, cookies, popcorn, napkins, pasta, and salad. There was also a green button for each team member, a visible token of the team's accomplishment in taking control and getting all the training done.

ESTABLISH A RELATIONSHIP

There must be alignment between vision and goals and the business creed and philosophy. Each business has a core philosophy that defines the culture of the organization. Sometimes this philosophy is published as its mission statement; sometimes it is not a written credo but is simply *lived* within the company. To implement an effective rewards and recognition system, it is important to be clear about the philosophy that drives your organization.

Address each of the following questions about your philosophy:

- Does the philosophy deal with the concept of recognizing the contributions made by employees? If so, how? _____

_____

_____

- Is the philosophy about recognition clearly stated? ___

  _____

  _____

- Is there harmony around recognition between what is
  written and what is lived?_____

  _____

  _____

There is a danger in having multiple messages. Organizations can have one written credo and a completely different de facto philosophy under which people operate.
For example, some organizations have a reward system in
place that touts the value of the contribution of all individuals in the organization. However, the reward system
is designed to give bonuses only to the top five percent in
the organization, which clearly contradicts the written,
teamwork-oriented philosophy.

The study of human behavior in organizations indicates
that the de facto message is much more important than
the professed, written one. The former is the one that truly
drives behavior. Does your organization have two
philosophies in operation? If so, what is the second, "real"
one? Once you can identify behavior drivers in the organization, you can begin to develop recognition-supporting
strategies. Is philosophical ambivalence an issue in your
organization? Can anything be done about it? How has
this affected recognition giving in your organization? Are
you willing and able to take the initiative to reduce any
dissonance that exists? Are you positioned to be a catalyst
for change?

The philosophy of the senior person or people in the organization influences organizational culture and must be
part and parcel of the vision and mission statements developed to drive the organization. Vision and mission established at the organizational level translate into operational

> The organization has a well-publicized, written philosophy that includes a statement about the value of recognition. Everyone knows it reflects the personal philosophy of the CEO. His participatory behavior supporting recognition, as defined in the philosophy, strongly affects how people reward one another. People in this organization *live* recognition. Employees are comfortable holding spontaneous events to recognize achievements of individuals and the group at large. A parade through the work area is not unheard of, and if he's available, the CEO will join it. Employees are quick to state that "valuing each person," "recognizing contributions," and "celebrating our successes" are reasons for the actions, and they often point out the recognition statement in the philosophy as justification for their spontaneous behavior.

goals and objectives at the individual level—that is, employees can use the corporate statements as screeners for personal behavior. If recognition is to be effective, its value must be voiced and demonstrated at the highest level and thus must be embodied in the documents that guide the organization.

Consider your own organization's vision: does it embody the following cultural elements?

- Open communication.
- Respect of individuals—their contributions and their self-worth.
- Openness to recognizing each person's contributions to the organization.

If you are lacking any of the elements identified above and you are not part of the strategy-making council in your organization, recognize that you will have difficulty in building support for a corporatewide recognition

process. As an alternative strategy to improving the state
of recognition giving in your organization, consider the
following basic options:

- Try to enlist a senior person to support your cause.
- Focus on your team environment—build recognition
  that the team can own and administer (as teams
  become more self-directed, they will be able to make
  more decisions around how they celebrate and
  recognize their contributions).
- Assume control of your own sphere of influence and
  see that you practice positive recognition behavior,
  regardless of the behavior of others in the
  organization.
- Take the NIKE approach and just do it. Introduce a
  recognition "program." Don't worry about process or
  strategy initially.

CLARIFY HOW GIVING RECOGNITION BENEFITS THE ORGANIZATION

If recognition is to be a strategy, there must be a clear value
added to the process, one that managers and individuals
can readily see. In the early stages of implementing a new
recognition strategy, not only must the recognition be
given, but its value must be verbalized. Individuals don't
always realize the relationships among the following:

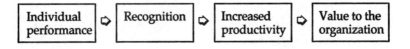

It is the responsibility of the leader to help clarify these relationships by saying "recognition equals value" and by taking a role that encourages others to participate. The leader must be quick to highlight positive examples of recognition being given within the organization. A very basic implementation strategy is to:

- Tell them what you are going to tell them about recognition.
- Tell them about what you want in the way of recognition behavior.
- Summarize what you told them about how and why recognition benefits the corporation.

This may seem simplistic and redundant, but by keeping it simple and repeating your message, you can make the strategy work.

One way of selling your ideas on recognition is to focus on the cost/benefit that the company will derive from the process. You might build a *T-account* (Table 2–1 is an example) to demonstrate what any type of recognition, particularly informal or spontaneous recognition, contributes to your company's bottom line. Some typical entries that might be included on both sides of such an equation are shown in Table 2–1.

Each of the entries in the T-account can be converted to actual dollar costs/savings for the organization. The bottom-line saving approach is useful when you are dealing with individuals who don't readily see the benefit of recognition. A dollar-oriented approach can demonstrate its impact in a visible, concrete way.

TABLE 2–1
Benefits and Costs of the Recognition Process

Benefits to Organization	Costs to Organization
Stress reduction in employees—laughter is a stress reducer and results in less time away from work caused by stress-induced illness.	Actual time spent in designing and implementing the recognition program or process.
Greater productivity—recognizing what you want results in more of the changed behavior being performed, and as a consequence productivity goes up.	The time it takes to give the recognition.
Positive mind-set—results in more time spent focusing on the job and less on complaining.	Dollars needed for whatever is given—this can be to provide supplies for make-your-own recognition and money spent for more formal media.
"Perk"-driven recognition—encourages greater productivity in both manufacturing and service environments; people like to work for tangible rewards.	The energy required to *teach* people how to give recognition, especially necessary if the environment doesn't currently support it.
Lower turnover.	The costs associated with instituting a new process.

CLEAR IMPLEMENTATION PLANS

To be successful, the strategy must be converted to written plans that are shared. The plan must ensure that recognition vehicles are available to everyone in the organization. The goal is that the recognition plan is embraced throughout the organization. This "embracing" is especially important when the plan incorporates a peer-to-peer focus. People don't want to get involved if they don't believe in or don't have a vested interest in the success of the plan.

Thought must also be given to who will take responsibility for the implementation of the strategy. It's very easy

An organization wanted to make sure that everyone had the opportunity to recognize others in a nonmonetary, spontaneous, light manner. To this end the company established a series of "recognition corners" throughout its complex, which were stocked with supplies so that employees could make awards for others. Sample ideas and awards were provided as models. The corners were located in easy-to-access spots that allowed some degree of privacy for the person creating the recognition.

for strategies and vision statements to be lost when individuals further down in the corporation don't see clear-cut ways to make the high-level ideas operational. Implementation plans must include the following:

- What is to be done.
- How it is to be accomplished.
- What resources are needed.
- Who will do what to make implementation happen.
- How funding and other costs are to be absorbed.

A CORPORATE CHAMPION

As stated earlier, making recognition a viable corporate strategy requires active support at the most senior levels within the organization. There needs to be one individual or a recognition team who claims ownership, who exemplifies the recognition-based behavior that the strategy supports, who makes sure that the support pieces needed to make the recognition plan work are in place, and who helps minimize the obstacles. Developing a champion takes time. Before you embark on your journey, ask yourself: Do I personally believe strongly enough in the

The recognition champion is the senior officer in the business unit. She is positioned to make things happen and has the respect of managers and individual contributors. People see what she *does*. She actively participates in the company's formal and peer recognition systems. Whenever something new is introduced, you can be sure that a person from her business unit will receive or give the reward. When things aren't right—when people aren't giving enough recognition or not using specific vehicles—she is positioned to see that needed changes occur. She personally finds out how different recognition options are received by participating and by walking around to see who is using what and to ask how people feel about different options. Not surprisingly, morale is consistently high in her unit, and it is one of the most innovative groups in the company.

value of recognition? Will I be able to put forth the energy that will be required to identify, recruit, educate, develop and support our champion? This simple self-test should be taken by the person or team who is charged with implementing a reward and recognition strategy in the organization.

The following questions can help you identify the person(s) who can best further the cause of all types of recognition within your company.

1. Who is a person(s) with an exemplary recognition pattern in your organization?
2. Who is in a role to influence the organization? How does the person's position enhance his ability to champion recognition?
3. What are some characteristics you would like to see in the person who acts as champion?

4. What strategy might you consider to approach your identified potential champion? Identify and decide how to sell the WIIFM.

5. What kind of support are you prepared to offer this person?

Evaluate your data and decide whether it is feasible to get the support you need from someone on your senior management team. If it is feasible, decide how best to proceed with recruiting and developing your champion. Remember, this person will be key to the overall design and implementation of your recognition strategy, so choose carefully.

- Name of a likely choice for champion? _____

  _____

- Briefly, what plan of action will you pursue to gain support of your champion?_____

  _____

Some of the barriers you will face in finding your champion are typified by the things people say when asked to support recognition:

- "I'm not comfortable giving recognition—I don't know how to give it."
- "I've never seen anyone who was good at giving recognition. How can you expect me to take a lead?"
- "Recognition is important, but it should be someone else's job to set a process or to administer whatever is in place."
- "It is important, but we don't have time to address it right now—we are too busy fighting daily fires."
- "My manager doesn't live it; therefore, it is something I can't be expected to live even though I believe in it."

If you agree there is merit in developing a champion and thus a recognition process, a first step is to help your management team recognize the value of recognition (especially spontaneous, nonmonetary recognition). Your goal is to convince a key person (potential champion and/or team) of the value of recognition in achieving the organization's vision and goals and to get that person to begin practicing appropriate recognition-based behaviors. If you can recruit the right person, recognition can become a part of your culture, albeit slowly. The following guide can help you take charge.

Taking Charge within Your Own Organization

Once you know your own organization, you will be ready to spend some time developing a strategy that can reasonably be expected to be implemented. The planning steps shown in the Strategy Planning Map can be used as a guide for developing your strategy.

Once you know what you want to accomplish, you will be ready to begin to assess your current state, regarding recognition. Identifying gaps between what you want and what you have will allow you to develop action plans for implementing recognition within your organization. If after reading this chapter you have decided that developing a rewards and recognition process isn't worth pursuing at this time, be clear and frank about why is this true. Regardless of the corporate position at the present time, are there things *you* can do to make recognition a part of your sphere of control? Think in terms of "you" and your sphere of influence as you read through the remainder of this book.

A Strategy Planning Map

Planning	Description of Step
Create a vision statement	Written in terms of the end result, what recognition will look like in your organization after you have implemented your system.
Develop supporting objectives	What your recognition strategy will accomplish for your organization.
Identify the critical success factors	Those elements that must be addressed and accounted for in order for the recognition process to succeed. Think in terms of who and what.
Determine probable obstacles	Those things that can get in the way of your recognition process succeeding. Think in terms of who and what.
Recruit the best champion for recognition in your organization	You must have an identified person or team if your initiative is to succeed. You must have their support before you begin.
Establish what the recognition process will include	What type of programs will need to be in place? Will they be management driven, peer-to-peer, formal and/or informal? See Chapter 7 for ideas.
Plan for the support systems that will need to be in place for it to work	Think in terms of who (people, departments) and types of support (training, materials).

Chapter 3

Measuring Current Recognition Patterns

Once you have developed a high-level strategy for recognition and you know where you would like to be (your vision or end state), you will need to determine what is in place today. Looking at today includes determining exactly what your company and team's current recognition state is and assessing your personal attitudes around giving and receiving recognition. This information will allow you to do a gap analysis as a basis for actual action planning.

CURRENT CORPORATE PATTERNS

Use the scale in Table 3–1 to determine your current recognition behavior (put an "x" in the appropriate box). If you are "in between" and one of the blank boxes reflects your current level, write in a definition of your present state.

Now, go through the list and check the box that reflects where you would like to be. The beginning point in gap analysis is both to define the desired and to identify the current state. Once you are clear about these two positions, you can begin to develop plans that will allow your organization to migrate (a gradual change) or shift (sudden, severe change) in order to reach the desired state. A systems approach to reward and recognition will include all types: formal and informal, management, team- and

TABLE 3-1
Scale of Corporate Recognition

Our Current State	Rating Scale	Description of Recognition Behaviors
	10	We live recognition—it is embedded in our culture. Everyone freely recognizes each other through a myriad of recognition vehicles that are in place within the organization.
	9	
	8	
	7	We acknowledge the importance of recognition in our business philosophy. There is a company-driven recognition program in place. In addition, some of us do the spontaneous peer-to-peer things.
	6	
	5	We are like the rest—there is a formal, company-driven recognition program in place and most people seem comfortable with it.
	4	
	3	We do a little—the company president gives some awards each year to recognize what we've done.
	2	
	1	Recognition? No need to recognize anyone—a true professional knows his or her own worth and doesn't need someone else talking about it!

individual-driven (a variety of categories and ideas to consider are included in Chapter 7). The gap analysis shown in Table 3–2 on pages 38 and 39 facilitates the assessment of your current and desired states. It can help you identify information needed to achieve any changes you plan. Spend energy in areas with the greatest gaps in order to reduce their gap size. Those areas with minimal gaps represent areas of strength within your organization—here your focus needs to be how to maintain high levels of performance.

The elements described previously can be evaluated (personally or through team effort) in light of your own organization and comprise the basic components of a recognition *process*, not a program. The difference between the two is critical. The former reflects a way of thinking and operating that includes active participation by everyone in the organization. The latter is a "token" doled out from above by management. In organizations that have a program, recognition is like all the other "show pieces"—it is simply something the organization touts as being in place. When it is a process, individuals experience and participate in the recognition. There is no need for corporate directives to continually highlight and explain how it works. It is embedded into the way people behave. It isn't a structured entity about which people assume an attitude that says, "OK, I've done recognition. Now I'm through with that. What will they do to me next?"

IDENTIFYING AND EVALUATING PERSONAL RECOGNITION PATTERNS

Once you have identified current patterns, assess what your measurement revealed. You will need to think at three distinct levels: (1) you—what you personally do in the recognition arena, (2) teams and peers—what others

around you in the organization do, and (3) company—
what corporate recognition is in place, and more impor-
tantly how employees support and use the system.

Personal Patterns

Patterns are reflections of typical behavior. When pooled
for all employees in the organization, they reflect the norm
and become what is defined as *culture*. The pattern evaluator checklist in Table 3–3 can help you reflect on the recognition that you personally give. Identify several
individuals (three to five minimum) to whom you have recently given recognition. Then, address the items with
those individuals in mind, going through the list for each
person named.

If you do not regularly give recognition, why don't you
make the effort? Each of the items in Table 3–3 will give
you some information about your personal recognition
patterns. The more times you responded "yes" the more
likely you are to give receiver-oriented recognition and
you are probably one who gives recognition on a regular
basis to many in the organization. (Note: This checklist can
be completed by a team to determine the focus and frequency of shared giving. The information can help the
team identify its strengths and weaknesses in recognition
giving. The ability to reward each other's contributions is a
critical success factor for teams.)

Whom did you choose? Think about the people you ref-
erenced when completing the checklist. Were they from all
levels of the organization, or did you select individuals primarily from one classification (peers, team members, subordinates, exceptional performers)? When recognition is a
process, people will recognize a variety of individuals at
all levels within the company.

A quick self check. When is the last time you recognized:
your boss, a co-worker or peer, your teammates (each of

TABLE 3-2
Recognition-Giving Gap Analysis

Elements to be Considered	Definition of Element	Description of Desired State	Description of Current State	PerceivedGap SizeBetween Desired and Current State*
Management-controlled/driven recognition	This includes formal approaches to reward and recognition. Typically these are programs which have specific rules that are set by management and that identify who can participate in the program and in what roles.			
Policies related to gift-giving	Because of tax implications, any gift-giving done in an organization must conform to tax regulations. This can influence who is able to give gifts that have a monetary value. It is important that the policies and procedures are written and understood by all.			
Team-based	This is recognition that is controlled by the team. What is given and any directive around the giving process is established by the team. No- or low-cost recognition is generally governed by the team. Recognition that requires company funding will have some boundaries set by the corporation.			
Peer-to-peer opportunities	Since most contact within an organization is with peers, it is important to encourage employees to recognize each other's contributions. Vehicles, whether no-cost and informal or formal and structured by the organizations, readily available to all employees.			

Low-cost/no-cost alternatives	The value of recognition is enchanced by recognizing things that the receiver values, by timing the recognition closely to the event. This category of rewards and recognition requires a variety of media that are accessible to everyone. It is a powerful tool in shaping employee contribution because it allows everyone in the organization to demonstrate, through rewards, what they prize in the way of work effort and product.		
Visibility—people at all levels giving recognition	Recognition becomes a process rather than a program when everyone is involved and all are empowered to give. Visibility reinforces involvement at all organizational levels.		
Accessiblity— the means to give are easily accessed by all	A formal recognition program is often inaccessible to most employees by virtue of the rules that govern it. A recognition *process* will include enough alternatives so that anyone can easily access some means of recognizing a co-worker in a timely and appropriate manner.		
Attention to quality	Rewards and recognition are in place to support quality within the organization. This includes focus on the customer, whether recognizing outstanding customer service or rewarding customers directly for their contribution to organizational process. Also recognized is attention to doing things "better, faster, cheaper."		

*Rate as minimal, moderate, or excessive.

TABLE 3–3
Personal Recognition Pattern Evaluator Checklist

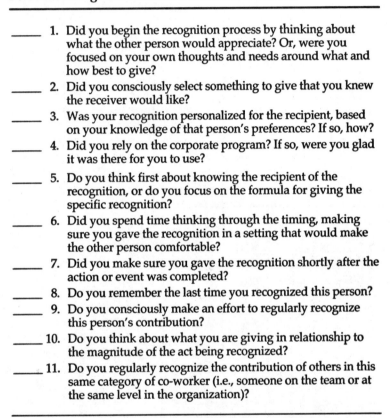

_____ 1. Did you begin the recognition process by thinking about what the other person would appreciate? Or, were you focused on your own thoughts and needs around what and how best to give?

_____ 2. Did you consciously select something to give that you knew the receiver would like?

_____ 3. Was your recognition personalized for the recipient, based on your knowledge of that person's preferences? If so, how?

_____ 4. Did you rely on the corporate program? If so, were you glad it was there for you to use?

_____ 5. Do you think first about knowing the recipient of the recognition, or do you focus on the formula for giving the specific recognition?

_____ 6. Did you spend time thinking through the timing, making sure you gave the recognition in a setting that would make the other person comfortable?

_____ 7. Did you make sure you gave the recognition shortly after the action or event was completed?

_____ 8. Do you remember the last time you recognized this person?

_____ 9. Do you consciously make an effort to regularly recognize this person's contribution?

_____ 10. Do you think about what you are giving in relationship to the magnitude of the act being recognized?

_____ 11. Do you regularly recognize the contribution of others in this same category of co-worker (i.e., someone on the team or at the same level in the organization)?

them should get recognition from you), a customer, or a supplier? In todays new organization, your long-term success is influenced by your ability to recognize and reward positive behavior in individuals in each of these groups.

You might say, "These were the first people I thought of and I recognize more people than this." This may be true, but our first impulses generally reflect our preferences. In other words, the people you wrote down reflect those you are most comfortable recognizing. If you regularly recognize a broader band of people than is reflected by the names you included, you might complete the checklist again using this broader base of people.

Were you able to easily identify three to five people? If you struggled to come up with names, there is a message for you. You might say, "I'm not positioned in the organization to give recognition. My boss limits me." This may be true regarding the use of formal recognition programs that are driven by senior management. However, we all can participate in spontaneous, informal recognition that focuses on the efforts of people in our immediate work unit and others we interact with. Did you remember that simply saying, Thank you, is a form of recognition? Including such a simple technique should make it easy for you to identify a minimum of three to five people whom you regularly recognize.

Tip

Your goal should be a breadth of recognition given within the organization. If you don't have it now, consciously think of people in different organizational units and plan some type of low-keyed recognition to acknowledge their contributions. If you haven't regularly participated in this type of recognition, it may be uncomfortable at first, but don't let that stop you.

What the Evaluator Checklist items tell us:

Items 1–4: These focus on the amount of thought that went into personalizing the recognition to the individual receiving it. When this is done, you reflect an appreciation that cannot be conveyed by formal company programs. Some people are willing to give but don't take the initiative to create or to personalize what is given. Recognition can be a spontaneous effort that relies on whatever is at hand. Its value to the recipient is the key to its worth.

Successful recognition givers maintain balance. If you answered yes to question four only, you are not getting personally involved, because you are relying solely on corporate recognition programs. This will be reflected in the recognition and can result in recipients not appreciating what was given because they sense you are removed. It can be a lose/lose—you gave and it wasn't appreciated, the recipient received and wished he hadn't been recognized, or at least not in the way it was done.

Personal gestures (i.e., saying thank you, a quick note, an invitation to coffee) of recognition tend to profile an individual who does more giving. Using the formal company program generally involves more bureaucracy, takes more effort, and is thus a slower procedure.

A Story

Samantha was an outstanding employee, and Joe wanted to recognize her efforts. Because Joe likes to be the center of attention and is very comfortable in groups, he arranged to have her receive the company's "Thank You" award at a companywide meeting. Her merits and contributions were outlined and everyone clapped because Samantha was truly a valuable employee. However, her closest friends cringed and felt truly sorry for her because she hated to be in the limelight and she was mortified by the recognition.

Moral

Knowing the person's feelings about recognition is more important than the recognition itself.

Items 5–7: These focus on the *context* of the giving. How much time elapsed between the event being recognized and the actual recognition? Was it done in private, within the team, or in a larger group? Just as important as thinking about what is being given is the factor of timing. People generally don't respect recognition that is given long after the event. When asked, most people will tell you that something small is preferential to a larger token that is given much later. Part of timing is where the recognition is given. When you give recognition, do you take the time to think about the setting? What is the behavior style of the person receiving the token? Do they like large groups? Are they a public or private person? As the story above revealed, you need to know about the person you are recognizing. Practice the Platinum Rule: Do unto others as they would like to be done unto.

Items 8–11: These address frequency. A key ingredient in your pattern is the frequency of your giving—to a specific individual as well as to a category of people in the organization. If you treat recognition as a process, you will have given a variety of rewards to lots of people at many different organizational levels. There will be both volume and breadth to your recognition. If you rarely give recognition, ask yourself why. Is it because:

- You don't know what people are doing on a daily basis?
- You consider recognition to be only for "big" contributions?
- You are uncomfortable with the process and thus avoid it?
- You buy into the philosophy that says, "People don't need to be recognized because they know intuitively when they are doing a good job?"

Each of the above practices creates a barrier to instituting recognition as a process. This is true at the individual level; and when the same thought patterns are harbored by many on the team or in the corporation, it begins to restrict giving behaviors in others.

What would ideal answers be to the questions included in the Evaluator Checklist? The goal of completing the checklist is to learn about yourself and your team's pattern of giving recognition. To that end, there is no one right answer to any of the items. The goal of your assessment is to help you establish a recognition process that demonstrates the following:

- A variety of recipients drawn from throughout the ranks of the company. This reflects broad-based giving and is found in a person or team attuned to the contributions of others in the company.

- A mixture in giving among options of informal, spontaneous recognition and formal company programs. Such a mix indicates an awareness of different recognition media and an understanding of the appropriateness of each option.

- A pattern of recognition in which the reward is given shortly after an event and in a breadth of environments. The breadth reflects the giver's sensitivity to the person receiving the recognition, as opposed to a giver who does what is comfortable or easy for herself.

- An abundance of recognition events. This would be reflected by the frequency of recognition and the breadth of people who have been recognized. If you are using low-cost or no-cost team-based and peer-to-peer types of recognition, the events should be occurring on an almost daily basis. Unless you aren't looking, it is almost impossible to go through a day without seeing something than can be recognized in a small, focused way.

Some people just naturally notice the things that others do. They are always taking the time to say, thank you to co-workers for a job well done. They do such things as: bring pizza to a crew that is working late, send letters home to thank the family when someone has put in extra work, or post complimentary letters received by employees so that all can share in recognizing a job well done.

TEAM-BASED AND PEER RECOGNITION-GIVING PATTERNS

Once you have established your own pattern of giving recognition, take some time to determine the patterns of others within your organization. Assume the mind set of your manager, some of your respected peers, and some team leaders and spend time identifying their patterns. The sample matrix in Table 3-4 can be used as a guide to assemble your data.

Are the patterns of the people you selected similar to yours? If you can't complete the matrix because you can't identify people you know enough about to be able to record their patterns, spend some time observing others. You should be able to list at least one person in each category (one exception is the subordinate category if you aren't in a management position). Observe the individuals long enough to be able to complete the matrix.

In light of the need to develop a strategy for recognition, one in which recognition is a process, consider what you

TABLE 3–4
Recognition Profiler

Person Observed	Specific Recognition the Person Gives that You Are Aware of	Who Are the Recipients? —by Name or Organizational Role	Do You Think of This Person as Giving a Great Deal or Minimal Recognition?	What Types of Recognition Does the Person Give Most? —Formal, Informal and so on
Peer				
Team leader or member				
Manager				
Subordinate				

learned by comparing the patterns you recorded in the preceding matrix. Are there things you can learn from those around you, things they are doing that you would like to adopt into your own behavior? Or, are you the one who can lead the organization in a more recognition-focused direction? You are doing things that you need to make others aware of if your organization is to be recognition focused. Your goal is to identify and analyze several points that you can take action on.

What are others doing in the way of recognition that you want to incorporate? It might be a specific recognition they give; it might be a type that you don't currently employ or might reflect a category of recipient that you don't now think of. _____

_____

_____

Can you identify gaps in recognition giving? If so, what can be done to improve your own or your team's performance to close the gap? _____

_____

_____

SYNTHESIZING RECOGNITION-GIVING PATTERNS

Based on what you have observed so far in yourself and others, can you identify a corporate pattern or strategy? If you are aware of a corporate pattern, describe it briefly—remember to do this in writing.

If you are unable to discern a pattern, consider the following possibilities:

- You haven't done enough homework and looked at the right people.

- You have looked and there is no identifiable strategy. Perhaps everyone is simply doing her own thing regarding recognition because the organization hasn't taken the lead in developing a strategy.

If you have characterized your organization as one in which everyone is operating under a different set of guidelines, you might not have collected enough information and are thus unable to discern patterns. Go through your organization chart and pinpoint key people. After observing these individuals, complete the Recognition Profiler matrix on page 46 for these people. Sufficient observation will allow you to discover your own corporate culture.

If, after careful observation, you determine that you do not have a clear or an acceptable pattern and you feel one is appropriate and feasible, you will need to backup to develop and implement that strategy. (Remember the importance of a champion.)

Another pattern to look for in recognition giving is outlined in the reward culture matrix in Figure 3–1. To complete the matrix:

1. Identify all the recognition programs you have in place in your organization today and record them in the appropriate boxes of the matrix (a program may fit in more than one box).

2. Identify as many people as you can in the organization who regularly give recognition and enter their names in the appropriate boxes (a person may appear in more than one box). If your organization is very large, you might think of groups of people based on some characteristic (grade level, role in organization, etc.) rather than individual names.

Ideally, people and programs will appear in most of the boxes. An inappropriate pattern would be all identified

FIGURE 3–1
Reward Culture Matrix

Identify people and programs within the company and place them in the boxes according to their classification as formal/informal and among the program driver categories.

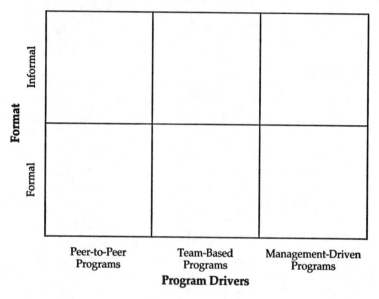

individuals and recognition falling into only one box or in one-half of the matrix. Having people in only a few boxes demonstrates imbalance at the individual level (people aren't able to adjust recognition to the situation). This would be true even if you were able to put a name into in each box but not have one name in several boxes. Also, your programs should be spread between both halves of the box and in all three driver categories. If you have programs in each box, you have a recognition system in place that can accommodate all employees.

Table 3–5
Evaluating Current Recognition Patterns

Patterns That Are-Aligned with Our Vision	Patterns That Will Need Change If We Are to Live Our Vision

MEASURING RECOGNITION IN LIGHT OF VISION

Go back and review the vision statement that you wrote as part of the strategy planning map, outlined in Chapter 2, page 33. Does what you learned in this chapter support or further that vision? To be successful your recognition patterns need to support your vision.

In Table 3–5, identify areas in which you are pleased with your current patterns and areas in which you will need to make changes in order to reach your vision end state.

Making changes to current patterns will not be easy. People operate within a comfort zone of behavior (regardless of its goodness or appropriateness) and they tend not to want to change. This is true for any change, whether initiated by the individual or driven by others. An additional dynamic is that a change in recognition-giving patterns by one or more individuals will ripple out and affect others in the organization. People will be impacted, comparisons between the old and new will be made, and motives for the changed behavior will be assumed. It is important that you understand the dynamics of the change process so that you can plan strategies to deal with the expected reactions. People can resist change even when it is for the better—for example, even though giving more recognition than was done before is positive, it may be resisted because it is something new.

Spend some time thinking through the changes you intend to make based on the patterns that emerged from the analysis of your personal, peer, team, and corporate assessments. Think in terms of present recognition-giving patterns and desired state and then develop plans to make the changes you wish and to deal with the probable outfall that the change to these patterns will cause. The following guide can help you with this process.

Proposed pattern change—from what to what?

Current: _____

_____

_____

Desired: _____

_____

_____

Who will be impacted and in what way?

Who: _____

_____

_____

How: _____

_____

_____

How will they react, in all probability? Create a:

Best case scenario: _____

_____

_____

Expected case scenario: _____

_____

_____

Worst case scenario _____

_____

_____

What can you do to mitigate any potential negatives?
Sequence planned events so that changes can be
introduced slowly and positively: _____

_____

_____

Whom can you enlist to support these changes?_____

_____

_____

How committed are you to actually following through on this change? (Unless you are totally committed, it is probably better to back off and rethink the change.) _____

_____

_____

Once you have determined the patterns that exist in your environment, you will be ready to look at the skills that will be needed in order to implement and maintain your plans.

Chapter 4

The Recognition Process: Skills Needed to Make It Happen

Giving recognition comprises both preference and skill. Some people are more attuned to thanking people; others feel that a thank-you, once said, will hold true for future related acts. Take the *What Is Your Preference* quiz on page 55 to get a sense of your preferences. Read each pair of words (from left to right) and then circle the word that sounds/feels most comfortable to you. Then, total the number of words you circled in each column and write the totals at the bottom.

If your number in the Column 2 was larger than the one in Column 1, you are probably more naturally attuned to recognition giving. It is a preference—you are more comfortable with the concepts and process. Notice we do not say you are more *skilled* at giving recognition. Giving recognition is a skill that can be cognitively learned and practiced. However, learning about your natural preferences provides knowledge to help you build recognition-giving skills that complement these preferred ways of behaving.

If you favored the words in Column 1, you will probably be happier with the recognition options included in the *left* column of Table 4–1. Likewise, if you favored Column 2, you will feel more comfortable with options in the *right* column in Table 4–1. Knowing your preferences lets you

What Is Your Preference?

Column 1	Column 2
Thinking	Feeling
Head	Heart
Objective	Subjective
Justice	Harmony
Cool	Caring
Impersonal	Personal
Critique	Appreciate
Analyze	Empathize
Precise	Persuasive
Principles	Values
Fair-minded	Warm-hearted
Truth	Tact
Firmness	Gentleness
Problem-solver	Cheerleader
Total: _____	Total: _____

develop personal strategies for recognition that rely on giving options that feel comfortable to you. Accommodating your preferences allows you to develop your skill level more easily.

Table 4–1 will help you think about differences in ways recognition might be given. The entries on the left are titled "thinking" options and are left-brained, less personal alternatives. The ones on the right are more personal, focusing on closeness, knowing another person, and doing something with a personal touch. As you read through the two lists, you will probably discover that one column or the other is more comfortable for you, representing things you would likely do or enjoy receiving. Ideally, you are skilled

TABLE 4-1
Recognition Options Based on Style Preferences

Thinking Options	Feeling Options
Write letters.	Shake hands.
Give recognition using the structured company program.	Provide spontaneous thank-yous.
Bring food: get doughnuts, buy a pizza.	Bring a handmade gift, e.g., make cookies or bake bread yourself.
Give gift certificates.	Take someone out for coffee or lunch.
Give a ready-made card.	Write a personal note.
Write an official memo to go into recipient's personnel the file.	Send a letter of thanks to the person and her family home.

From past experience, Judy knows she belongs on the "right side." She naturally recognizes people. At work she invites others to lunch, brings in little gifts to say thank you, and makes sure that people have the things they need to do their job before they ask. She rarely uses "formal" types of recognition, and even when she uses these she adds a personal touch—for example, she gives a bonus and includes a personalized pen to endorse the check with. Because of her participation on the team planning for the formal company awards dinner, in addition to formal awards given within company guidelines, everyone who attended received a token gift to thank them for coming. Whenever and wherever she is involved, people never lack for recognition.

at pulling from both lists, depending upon the person being recognized. (Remember the Platinum Rule.) Knowing which side is more comfortable helps you plan and will make recognition giving more successful. When you give recognition that is less comfortable (pulled from the column you prefer less), you will need to plan more and do the giving in a "safe" environment (someplace where you are comfortable).

As you read through the recognition-giving skills discussed below, think in terms of yourself—decide how comfortable you are with each skill. The more comfortable you are with a skill, the easier it will be to practice. Since skill development takes practice, you will need to create specific action plans to increase your effectiveness in the interpersonal skills basic to recognition giving. For uncomfortable skills, allow for more practice and make sure your initial attempts are done in a safe setting, that is, recognize people who won't judge you or affect your job.

Tip

Whenever you are working at developing a skill that is not particularly comfortable, try to do it using a recognition medium that plays to your preferences. Example: If you favored the behavior patterns in the left column of the *What Is Your Preference* quiz, then select recognition options in the left column of Table 4–1. Do early giving to someone who you think prefers the same side of the table as you do.

It is much easier to develop skill when you are in your comfort zone and have the support of your strengths to help with the development process.

BASIC RECOGNITION-GIVING SKILLS

There are several basic skills that everyone needs to develop in order to be an effective giver of recognition, regardless of one's position in the company or one's giving preferences. Your goal is to become an effective recognition giver who truly enjoys the opportunity to interact with other employees. Hopefully you will learn to acknowledge the contribution made by each team member/peer and freely give recognition. Regardless, you need to learn to observe and listen carefully to the individuals you are recognizing.

A technique that some successful givers use (one that helps those less naturally attuned to giving) is to build a file indicating the preferences of individuals within their sphere of recognition. Examples of how this is applied:

- John knows that Amanda doesn't like anything that is too personal. He makes sure that any recognition she receives is fairly formal, impersonal, and given in private without a handshake or a pat-on-the back.

- Mary knows that Joe appreciates the opportunity to sit and chat and be in the limelight. Recognition for him needs to be much more personal—maybe an award presented in front of the entire team with lots of fanfare and handshaking.

- Scott knows that when recognizing someone for the first time, it is important to be aware of the reactions of the person being recognized. He is very conscious of body clues. In the future he uses this information to tailor the recognition specifically to a person. The result: people value the recognition they receive and will tell you that Scott is a person who sure knows how to make a person feel worthwhile.

OBSERVATIONAL SKILLS

Also necessary to effective recognition giving are observational skills—the ability to "watch" in order to learn about others. This includes observing work products and processes, since these are the bases for any recognition that is given in the workplace. Also a part of the observation process is noticing and reading the nonverbal messages that help one determine what kind of recognition will be most positively received. (Recognition is most powerful when you recognize a contribution that the other person values.)

Application. Effectively using one's observational skills includes the following:

1. Watch a person's body when he is describing a work product. Some examples of things to look for in the other person:

- Posture—standing a little taller, which reflects that he feel good about what he has done.
- Gestures—are more animated.
- Eye contact—is more direct.

2. Be alert to clues from past recognition. If someone values and appreciates a token of recognition he or she has received, it will remain visible. This is why you frequently see the tokens that people have given each other posted or left out in the work space. When you see such a token displayed, find out what was recognized; this represents the type of contribution you also would want to recognize. Be sure that you take the time to compliment the person on having received the recognition that she or he keeps visible. This in itself is a form of reward.

3. Notice how a person reacts to any recognition that is given. Reactions can include how the receiver responds

> The company initiated a new recognition program in which building blocks were given as recognition tokens for exceeding quotas. It became an informal, collegial competition among the staff to see who could build the highest structure.

to: the person doing the giving, what was given, and how it was done. Is there a "leaning into" the giver, suggesting pleasure, or does the body slump over or withdraw, indicating that the person is not pleased with what or how it is done?

You can assess your comfort and skill levels with observational skills by using the check sheet on page 74.

LISTENING SKILLS

A giver of recognition should also cultivate good listening skills. Part of the listening process is to hear the message that the receiver gives you about how she is reacting to the token and the process. As the giver, you must learn to use the information gained by active listening to enhance the recognition process in the future.

Application. Effective listening requires that the giver consciously watch his own body during the recognition process and also pay attention to the receiver. Some of the manifestations of good listening include:

1. Being aert to the tone of the message—38 percent of any face-to-face communication is carried by a person's voice tone. The giver must be alert to her own tone and also listen for any messages conveyed by the recipient through his tone.

F

Components of Active Listening

1. **Attending behaviors.** These are all the nonverbal messages that a listener gives to help communicate his thoughts and/or feelings. Attending behaviors include such things as: maintaining eye contact, leaning toward the other person, facing the other person, speaking in a pleasant, convincing voice, and observing general rules of body movements.

   Example: You say, "Thank you for a job well done," everything in your voice, posture, and facial expressions also says, "Thank you," and the receiver accepts it openly—doesn't cross arms, frown, or step back. Appropriate attending behaviors minimize the potential for mixed messages— having memorized the right words but not demonstrating the right physical message. Mixed messages result in loss of honesty in communication as well as credibility.

2. **Paraphrasing** This is listening to what the receiver says (verbally and nonverbally) in response to the recognition, and then verbalizing one's own observations or perceptions of the acceptance. This process helps you clarify how the recognition was received so that future awards can be most appropriate to the individual's style.

   Example: The manager who stops by a week after the recognition was given to comment, "Jon, I noticed that you were all smiles when you got the certificate last week. I see you still have it up. Receiving it must have made you feel pretty good. I'm glad you liked it, and I know I appreciate your contribution to the project and was glad I could acknowledge your efforts."

continued

Be prepared also to reflect when you observed a recognition that was not particularly appropriate. Think through how you will handle such a potential situation before it occurs.

Example: Don, I really appreciate your contribution to the project. I noticed that you were very reserved and weren't smiling when I gave you the certificate. Would there have been a better way for me to acknowledge how much I appreciate all the skill you bring to our team? If you can think of anything you are willing to share, please let me know. I'd like to be able to let you know how much I appreciate all the good work you do, and I'd like it to be right for you.

3. **Addressing feelings**—both yours and the receiver's. Until you put yourself in the receiver's shoes, you cannot understand her feelings, and you won't be as effective as a giver of recognition. Focus on what the receiver is feeling—look for body language clues. Identify your own feelings about the giving process. Again, be prepared to deal with negative feelings. Sometimes when we try out a new process or recognize someone for the first time, we aren't perfect. Being open to acknowledging this and planning to do something with the information helps to improve future effectiveness.

2. Demonstrating attending skills—these define how one listens. Most of the skills are simple and quick, as described in the box above.
3. Practicing nonverbal attends—these are the nods and "noises" that one makes to *show* that one is listening.

4. Paraphrasing—verbalizing the giver's perception of the receiver's reaction to the recognition in order to verify that the giver accurately understood those reactions.

You can assess your comfort and skill levels with listening skills by using the check sheet on page 74.

WHIMSY

Also essential to giving recognition is allowing yourself to have fun. Too many people in the business community discount the importance of laughter and fun. Because of its power to break down barriers and reduce stress, laughter should be encouraged as a part of the reward system.

Example: The team completed the project ahead of time and under budget because everyone pulled more than their own weight. To celebrate they had T-shirts made that said "We Are Awesome". They wore them to work on Fridays for an entire month. The team laughed at its egotistical statement, and they were good-naturedly ribbed by others in the department. Their reward was casual dress days and the opportunity to show off their accomplishments in a way that made everyone laugh.

Recognition can be even more powerful as a motivator when it takes on an air of whimsy. This does not mean that those involved think it unimportant; instead it means that an important part of the "thank you" message needs to be cloaked in a blanket that allows those involved to enjoy the experience.

Application. Use the following self-checks to examine your degree of whimsy:

1. Count the number of times you laugh with someone during the recognition-giving process. If it's all formality and seriousness, think about ways to build in laughter. This laughter needs to be hearty and sincere, based on a shared feeling of goodwill, not the nervous laughter of someone who is doing something he doesn't like or is uncomfortable with.

2. Seek out stories to tell. Do some exploration into the person receiving the recognition. Look at yourself. Can you find something to make light of the situation that will draw laughter and enhance the value of the contribution?

Kris was being recognized for her role in the project. While giving her the bonus she deserved, the manager spent some time laughingly recounting the snacks she keeps and how they kept her going. He recounted the time she had a jar of trail mix and was caught by the team eating only the banana chips—they knew what she was up to because they could hear her crunching away in her cubicle during one of the team's middle-of-the-night sessions. The more she concentrated, the louder the crunching.

---

3. Look for something humorous in the occurrence itself—some piece that all can reminisce and laugh about.

You can assess your comfort and skill levels with whimsy skills by using the check sheet on page 74.

SENSITIVITY

Caring for others is crucial to the recognition process. Some people have a natural sensitivity to the feelings and reactions of those around them; others must work at learning to watch and react. This is the concept of "walking a mile in someone's shoes." Recognition is best when it meets the needs of the receiver. To do this effectively you must be able to understand and be sensitive to the other person and let her know of your empathy.

Tish loves a party and likes recognition that involves lots of people getting together to celebrate. However, she knows her co-worker, Steve, is uncomfortable in groups. To recognize his outstanding customer service skills, she wrote him a nice letter and sent it with a special book to his home.

Application. An example of this skill would be your learning to ask yourself periodically throughout the recognition process: "What is the receiver seeing, thinking, feeling right now? What specific behaviors am I picking up on? What can I do to accommodate the needs of the receiver?" Unless you are naturally sensitive, this is a skill area that takes a great deal of effort to develop because it requires you to focus your energy outward rather than inward. You will know if you have this natural ability because of previous experiences such as people telling you about your outstanding sensitivity in reading and understanding others.

You can assess your comfort and skill levels with sensitivity skills by using the check sheet on page 75.

SYSTEM-DRIVEN SKILLS

There are certain company-related skills that managers and leaders must demonstrate if recognition is to be successfully implemented within an organization.

Knowledge of the "Formula"

This is knowing specifically *what* to say to keep the recognition focused. When giving recognition there are a few points that the giver needs to remember to include. They comprise a formula or recipe that an effective giver of recognition needs to memorize. However, the giver must be able to personalize it to the recipient to be effective. In some instances, it makes sense to write out and practice what you will say before giving, especially if you rarely give recognition and/or are uncomfortable with the process.

Application. The following are the elements that you want to include in your recognition recipe. How you sequence them will depend upon your style. Just be sure to include all points.

Recognition-giving recipe
- Thank the person by name.
- Specifically state what was done that is being recognized. Specificity is extremely important because it identifies and reinforces the behavior you want more of.
- Explain how the behavior made you feel. Include this step only if you can be honest in the feelings you are reflecting.
- Point out the value added to the team or company by the behavior.
- Thank the person by name again for his or her contribution.

"Don, thank you for taking the time to call on those 10 extra customers last week. I know that it required you to work 10 extra hours, and I'm personally very appreciative of your effort. This type of contribution will ensure that we exceed our profit plan for the quarter and this means that everyone will get a bonus. Again, Don, thank you for all your hard work."

Covering the basic points in the statement you make lets you get your message of thanks across in a concrete and honest way. Saying thank you is a powerful recognition, and it can be done quickly, easily, and immediately. The verbal acknowledgment is appreciated by the recipient and doesn't require a "gift" to be attached. It is always surprising how many people will identify this type of recognition as a desired form and one that they don't hear often enough.

Awareness of Company Program

If you are positioned to use the company program for recognition, be sure you understand the program and use it to advantage. It is the responsibility of those who can access the company program to use it to its fullest. (If the company program includes discretionary bonus dollars, be sure they are used fully. When dollars are available but not used, employees quickly understand that the organization doesn't believe in recognizing its employees.)

- Know the culture around using the program.
- Make sure you recognize as many individuals as you can through the vehicles available.
- Encourage those you manage also to use the program—do this verbally and through modeling.

Each member in the organization is allocated dollars to be spent on recognition. Quarterly spending is tallied by team and the results shared. This is done as percentage of dollars available rather than by actual dollar amounts so that units aren't focusing on "how much" each got but instead on how they make use of the dollars available to them. It has become somewhat of a competition among units to see that their percentages are high.

Application. As part of the management training process, individuals should be expected to learn about any recognition programs the company has in place. An organization serious about recognition will also measure the effectiveness of its management team by how much they use the recognition programs that are in place. Managers are often uncomfortable giving recognition and will avoid doing so unless there is some sort of motivator to see that they get involved. It is the company's responsibility to encourage its members to give recognition. To this end, the organization must be prepared to provide the necessary skills training to the leaders of the organization.

Timeliness, the Platinum Rule, and the Appropriateness of What Is Given

All of these issues can be reduced to cognitive "formulas" that ensure that the recognition is done effectively. Managers must think about each of these elements and then make sure that any recognition they give addresses these elements. Because they can be addressed in structured ways, there is really no excuse for individuals not to apply the elements correctly.

Application.   A company that does recognition well will take steps to see that managers know how to deal with each of the elements. This can be accomplished through training sessions. It can also be addressed by providing each manager or team with an appropriate recognition-giving handbook that provides formulas and checklists to help individuals deal appropriately with the recognition process. Once these tools are in place, managers and teams can be measured in part by how well they recognize the contributions of their work team members. The measurement gives greater credence to the importance of recognition. Unless the performance management system reinforces giving recognition, it will not be done on a widespread basis.

Timeliness
In our organization recognition will be given within one week of the event.

Platinum Rule
We will always take the time to ask, "What will the receiver appreciate most?"

Appropriateness
We will think through the relationship between what is given and the act. This means that we will make greater use of nonmonetary options because they reinforce specific behaviors and lend themselves to a breadth of contribution.

You can assess your comfort and skill levels with system-driven skills by using the checklist on page 75.

PEER-TO-PEER SKILLS

There are also skills that individual contributors and team members must demonstrate if they are to effectively take ownership for recognizing the efforts of co-workers. It can be argued that these skills need to be developed within individual contributors regardless of corporate positioning around recognition.

Honest Appreciation of Others

Honest appreciation reflects a level of respect that is achieved after people work together long enough to recognize the strengths and weaknesses each member brings to the team. It also demonstrates a high level of peer knowledge, an appreciation of how members contribute, and an openness to recognizing contributions. Respect and appreciation reflect attitudes within individuals, ones that can be addressed and improved through training. To address them, you must allow for the time it takes to build a culture in which people are comfortable enough to demonstrate appreciation freely for one another.

Application.   Group discussion around what work team members value in each other is a beginning point for building respect and honesty. Sessions can be held for employees to discuss topics such as:

- What we bring to the table.
- What I respect and value in other team members.
- What I value in my own contribution.
- How to show appreciation in a way that matches team needs.

These topics will encourage individuals to begin to talk about strengths and developmental needs of team members in an open and honest way and can lead to planning for the required skill building.

Everyone recognized the need to let one another know what was working and what needed to be changed. To address the need-to-change areas, the team developed the "Blooper of the Week" award. It was given on Friday at the team's weekly round-up meeting to let team members know about something that was poorly done. Specific "might-have-considered-doing-differently" items were written on the award certificate. Over time, everyone received an award, so no one was offended when it was his turn. It provided an easy way to humorously and behaviorally identify teammates' actions and behaviors that needed to be modified.

Open Communication among Team Members

Also necessary is an open environment in which people are able to share their appreciation for one another's contributions. This requires specific communication skills that can be taught—listening, command of one's own body language messages, sensitivity to meta-language, and so forth. In addition, open communication requires a culture high in trust. Such an environment is characterized as one in which team members know they can express both their positive and their constructive messages openly and not fear reprisal. Open communication environments are replete with creative recognition that is spontaneous, creative, light, and relaxed, among other things.

Application. Teaching people to communicate openly is a long-term effort. The beginning point is to teach communication skills that will allow individuals to begin dialoguing about what they see. Start with recognition that focuses on what members respect in one another.

Then, introduce tools to constructively identify things that might be improved upon (never look at what is *wrong*). Open communication is a cultural issue. Modeling the desired behavior must begin at the top of the organization.

Creativity—Keeping It Simple, Cheap, Quick

People need to learn that simple recognition sincerely given is the most valuable. Organizations can encourage creative recognition by providing examples of what is wanted, seeing that materials are available to support the initial recognition ideas, and rewarding employees who are willing to risk being creative.

The organization wanted to get people more involved in spontaneous, no-cost recognition. A recognition booth was set up with lots of colored paper, glitter, felt pens, stars, stickers, and so on. People were encouraged to take advantage of the booth, and the managers supported the time they spent "creating" their own recognition to give "freely."

Application.   It is the responsibility of the organization to help employees learn about simple-to-use ideas and to make readily available the material needed to give this type of recognition. Organizations can provide workshops, notebooks, or articles in the company newsletter or post examples of the type of recognition being encouraged. People will be much more likely to get involved when they have clear ideas of what they can give. Once involved, the creativity will begin to grow naturally because people will discover the fun in the process. This will be enhanced by a leadership style that encourages the creativity by recognizing those who have given creative recognition to others.

You can assess your comfort and skill levels with peer-to-peer skills by using the check sheet on page 76.

HOW TO DEVELOP THESE SKILLS

Learning how to give effective recognition takes work. A good beginning step is to complete the skills matrix below. This will help you determine gaps in your skills. What areas are important to you, the team, and/or the organization? How comfortable are you with your skill in those areas ranked high? Large gaps are important if the skill is highly valued; spend energy to improve in these areas. If gaps are small, you know you are on target, so keep doing those things that are highly valued. Maintain your efficiency in these areas and periodically check to see if skill-level remains high or if change is needed. Don't emphasize or put much energy into those areas with low rankings, regardless of gap size. Assess your skill in each of the skill categories addressed throughout this chapter. Use the matrix below to do a self evaluation—this can be for self, team, and/or organization. Determine your own/team's/organization's level of comfort or skill with each of the recognition-giving skills described within the chapter.

After you have completed and analyzed your responses, use the information to develop an action plan using the guide that follows to ensure that you developed the skills needed within your organization. If your team or organization isn't ready, you can complete the planning exercise for yourself.

TABLE 4–2
Skill Matrix

Skill Area	Score						Ranked Importance of Addressing the Skill	
	Current			Desired			To You	To the Team/ Organization
	H*	O*	L*	H*	O*	L*		
Observational Skills Attuned to body language in others.								
Aware of clues from the past about preferences in recognition.								
Watch and read reaction in receiver to recognition that is given.								
Listening Skills Alert to the tone of the message in both the giver and receiver.								
Demonstrating attending skills.								
Practicing nonverbal attends.								
Paraphrasing.								
Whimsy The number of times you laugh with someone during the recognition-giving process.								
Seek out stories to tell.								
Find the humor in the occurrence itself.								

TABLE 4–2 *(continued)*

Skill Area	Score						Ranked Importance of Addressing the Skill	
	Current			Desired			To You	To the Team/ Organization
	H*	O*	L*	H*	O*	L*		
Sensitivity Conduct periodic self-checks to maintain focus on receiver rather than self.								
Consciously focus on behaviors and feelings of the receiver—the goal is to identify specifics.								
Awareness of own level of natural sensitivity to needs of others as demonstrated in recognition giving.								
System-Driven Skills Knowledge of and comfort with using the Recognition-Giving Recipe.								
Awareness of the company program— understanding of and willingness to use.								
Ability to apply knowledge of appropriate timing, the Platinum Rule, and appropriateness of what is given to ensure that recognition is successful.								

TABLE 4–2 (concluded)

Skill Area	Score						Ranked Importance of Addressing the Skill	
	Current			Desired			To You	To the Team/ Organization
	H*	O*	L*	H*	O*	L*		
Comfort with Peer-to-Peer Skills Demonstrating an honest appreciation of others and providing for the development of this attitude in all employees.								
Fostering an environment that encourages open communication among team members.								
Encouraging creativity in employees in ways of giving recognition that are simple, cheap, and quick.								

*What do the specific comfort-level scores mean?

High (H)   This is an area of strength and comfort in giving recognition. You want to do more in this skill area when possible because of the return on effort.

Okay (O)   This is an area in which your performance is adequate but you feel you can improve. Look for patterns of behavior—your strengths and developmental needs. (Example: You are comfortable recognizing peers but have a great deal of difficulty with subordinates.)

Low (L)   This is an area of recognized weakness in which you need to develop skill. Take the time to practice these skills in a controlled environment. Get help through training and coaching. Learn to observe those who are effective in this skill area; use them as models.

Your goal is to develop a strategy to ensure that the identified skills help to achieve the short- and long-term recognition strategies that you established earlier. Determine the following:

1. Where are you now?
   - Can you address the basic skills with everyone in the organization?
   - Will you need to target specific groups (e.g., must you concentrate on developing your managers or leaders first so that they can model for others in the organization)?
2. Have you established a hierarchy for addressing the reward and recognition processes? Do you know what should be addressed first, based on your organization's culture and on the people within the organization?

Once you know your current state and the gaps that exist between it and the desired skill level especially for skills areas that were identified as important, you can begin to formulate plans for the development of the skills that will ensure that recognition works—for you, for your team, and for your organization. The following guide can help you develop your action plans. The points that are highlighted, when addressed, will increase your likelihood of following through on your action plans and thus increase the probability of your establishing a successful recognition system.

Recognition Skills Development—Action Planning

Identify one skill you want to work on. _____

_____

_____

Who will need to develop this skill? Be specific in your description—name the managers, individuals, and team members who will be the focus of your action. _____

_____

_____

_____

How, specifically, will this skill help the target audience to give more effective recognition? _____

_____

_____

_____

What type of contribution will be focused upon? Being clear on this will help later with the behavioral explanation and the measurement of the skill. _____

_____

_____

_____

What recognition media are available to you currently within the organization? _____

_____

_____

_____

Select one and then explain why you chose to use that one. Be sure it matches your comfort level for giving and that it is appropriate to the recognition-giving skill you want to develop. _____

_____

_____

_____

What will be the hardest part of the skill development process? What will create the greatest obstacles to your success? Be specific in your description. _____

_____

_____

_____

How will you know how well you are doing at developing the skill you are focusing on? Develop a measurement tool that you can use. Examples: a self check, getting feedback from others (identify whom you will ask and what you will ask them). _____

_____

_____

_____

What is your time frame for this action? By when will you have accomplished your goal for skill improvement?_____

_____

_____

_____

You have just identified at least one specific recognition-giving skill that you plan to develop. You are now ready to look at specific ways by which you can institute recognition within your organization to capitalize on and develop the attitudes, strategies, and skills you have identified and deemed important. You will need to develop a program or process that will work within your organization. The next chapter provides a model that can help you institute a system that will work for you.

Chapter 5

Establishing a Model Program

After establishing the commitment level to recognition and determining individuals' comfort with, and skill in, the process, the actual program or process, can be implemented. Basically, the implementation flow is as follows in Figure 5–1.

These are the steps to follow to establish a recognition system. As you read through the material in this chapter, think in terms of where you and your organization currently are and where you wish to be—your vision or end-recognition state. Remember: If the organization isn't ready to address recognition as an organizationwide system, you can still adopt a recognition focus in your own behavior.

STEP 1: ESTABLISHING THE FOUNDATIONS FOR RECOGNITION IN THE ORGANIZATION

The following are some of the questions that help set the direction for a recognition system. They must be addressed by the decision makers during the planning process.

- Will the process be management driven?
- Will it focus on a team-based or peer-to-peer process?

FIGURE 5–1
Steps to Establishing a Recognition System

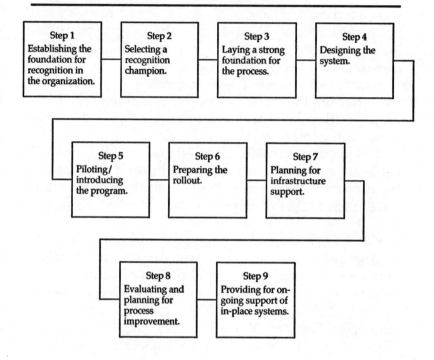

- Will there be some effort to include multiple types of recognition?
- How will the different facets be introduced, in what sequence, and how will they complement each other?
- What measures will be in place to let us know we are successful?

The most common form of recognition is the management-controlled, formal recognition program. This type of program is a positive first step on the recognition journey. It allows individuals in the organization to begin to acknowledge the importance of rewards and recognition and it sanctions their role in the organization. Most corporately controlled programs are governed by rules established by a management team and published in the company's management handbook. Read through the recognition guidelines for almost any organization, and you will find topics such as the following:

• Criteria for reward and recognition—these identify the behaviors the organization wants to recognize. To be most effective these need to be tied in to the values and norms of the corporation.

• Managerial considerations—these provide the philosophical justification for reward and recognition as part of the corporate HR system. They focus on things such as recognition's role as a movitator, how to give recognition, benefits of recognition, and so forth.

• How to nominate someone for an award—in most management driven programs, employees may *suggest* but only management has the *right to grant*. Processes range from those with a great deal of protocol involved, to others in which fairly simple "tokens" are readily available to all employees. The key difference among programs is generally the power to grant. There is not necessarily a correlation between dollars and opportunity to give—in some organizations the most coveted award can be a pin, a plaque, or a name on a wall.

• Types of recognition available within the organization—most organizations that have formal, management-driven programs have them set up as hierarchical. A quick read-through of program guidelines will verify that rewards are categorized by management levels and that there is a correlation between the dollar value or importance of the award and the position in the hierarchy of those who may access the recognition.

• How to deal with monetary implications—for any cash award, taxes and budgeting issues exist and organizations must have policies to address them. For this reason, some organizations favor nonmonetary rewards.

An organization interested in establishing or revising a management-driven program can reference a variety of resources. There are written materials that can be used as models or shells for such programs and there are consulting organizations prepared to come in and set up or help an organization set up its own program.

Management-driven programs are an important piece of the recognition mosaic but are not the only piece. Organizations are also wise to look to team-based and peer-to-peer recognition. When you consider that most employees spend 90 percent of their interaction time with their teams and peers, you begin to appreciate the importance of individuals acknowledging each other's contributions. Today's migration to teams also impacts the need for recognition and reward systems that address giving among members.

It is not enough to rely on people taking the initiative to recognize each other, hoping that they will have the knowledge and tools to do this and to do it in the right way. In light of today's focus on workplace redesign, with the increased reliance on self-directed and virtual teams, successful organizations will need to build team and peer recognition into their organizational culture. Reward and recognition is part of the process of building teams into the organizational structure.

What will such programs include? Traditional elements of recognition programs, such as modeling by key people and the provision for time and materials, need to be included. New issues are those of spontaneity, playfulness, informality, and equality. Since these are less familiar to and less comfortable for most employees, more consideration will need to be placed on these elements of successful team-based recognition.

Some questions to consider as you establish a foundation for rewards and recognition in your organization include the following:

What are the core recognition drivers for your organization or team?

What kind of focus will the program you set up in your organization have?

Who will be the primary target audience for controlling, giving, and receiving recognition?

STEP 2: SELECTING A RECOGNITION CHAMPION

Today's organization with its constantly changing priorities must have an identified *champion of recognition* for it to maintain visibility and importance. If you were to poll people about the value of recognition, they would certainly identify recognition as being important to employee motivation. Yet the realities of constant fire fighting and changing priorities usually mean that actual attention to giving recognition gets less priority than most people would say it deserves. A way of countering this reality is by identifying a highly visible and powerful champion, someone whose modeling of recognition will give it enough credence that people begin to take the time to use the recognition vehicles that are available. Be sure you recruit an active champion, one who will do more than take on the job in name only.

The following questions will help you identify a champion in your organization:

What specifically do you require of your champion?

Who can fill this role in your organization? Begin with several potential candidates.

To Ponder

If you find that your champion is not active or is otherwise inappropriate, are you positioned to take necessary action to replace that person? If you will be "stuck" with whomever you choose, be sure that you recruit wisely. This generally means checking out track records of individuals you are considering and spending time explaining in detail exactly what will be required in terms of effort, time, role, and so forth. Understand that you may have to do more behind the-scenes work to support some people than you would have to do for others. Be prepared to position and support your champion so that she is visible as the doer while you are taking care of the behind-the-scenes work that makes things happen.

Who among the candidates is the best person for the role?

How will you gain the support of this person?

STEP 3: LAYING A STRONG FOUNDATION FOR THE PROCESS

High-level parameters for recognition, such as the following, must be set by senior management:

- The company's dollar commitment to the process.
- An agreement reached by consensus to support actively whatever process is implemented.
- Decisions about what kinds of recognition are to be in place (management-driven, team-based, or peer-to-peer). Do we want it to be public or private? Will the recognition be monetary, nonmonetary, or both?

(Note: Senior management should set the direction, not make decisions about the program specifics. For example, they would not decide whether to give dollar bills, pins, plaques and so on.

- Establishing who will participate in the giving process: Is it to be high-level executives only? Will all managers participate? Or will it be open to teams and individual contributors?

- Designing the mechanics of the financial considerations: Are program dollars managed at the top? Are they set up as discretionary funds that can be governed within work areas?

These types of decisions or parameters are best set *before* actual program or process design begins. Find out what is important to individuals in the way of reward and recognition. This will ensure that what is included matches employee expectations.

Recognition is most effective when those who will live the process are involved in its design. However, the high level macroparameters of the program or process must be set and owned by senior management. Once set, they will serve to define the philosophy that will guide the future design of the actual recognition system in the company.

An example of parameters is illustrated in the recognition vision statement in the box on page 87.

STEP 4: DESIGNING THE SYSTEM

An annotated version of the vision statement can be used by the design team as a litmus test to determine whether a program element is appropriate. The goal is not to take the

Vision Statement
As an organization, we are quick to value and to recognize each other's contributions. We ensure that efforts are recognized and rewarded in an appropriate and timely manner.

Such a vision (part of the overall business philosophy statement), established by senior management, could be translated for or by the design team. Consider some of the key messages included in this sample vision statement:

We as an organization implies more than the current, typical situation in which managers recognize and reward employees when they see them performing in exemplary ways or when they are told about performance. The implication is that *all* employees need to be sensitive to the contributions being made by each person. All individuals must be empowered and willing to take the initiative to see that co-worker efforts are recognized.

Assure that efforts are recognized and rewarded means that employees who *want* to give recognition are afforded the means to do so. Opportunity doesn't necessarily equate to dollars. Instead, it implies that the tools and ideas for recognizing each other are in place and that the culture supports people taking the initiative to give the recognition.

In an appropriate and timely manner recognizes that there is no one reward that fits all. It is the responsibility of the organization to provide a broad range of recognition devices and ideas that employees can draw upon to match a particular recipient's effort. Timeliness is important to most recipients. It is the responsibility of the design team to see that vehicles are incorporated so that rewards can be given in an appropriate time frame.

If the design team interprets the statement, they must verify their interpretation with senior management before taking action.

design process away from the team but instead to set boundaries. Simply providing a vision statement is not sufficient direction from the top because of the opportunity for interpretation. The team's perception of the statement may not coincide with that of senior management and thus may negate the work done by the team.

The best design team, the one most able to get company-wide support for the recognition sytem is a cross-level team.

The job of the cross-level design team is to:

- Decide what the program or process should look like.
- Determine what needs to be included.
- Detail how provisions for the desired recognition are to be provided and accessed.

If the organization is truly committed to implementing lasting recognition, there must be employee involvement in the design process. The opportunity to decide *how* to recognize effort within the organization will affect how employees value the recognition process and affect their willingness to participate proactively in the process.

The design team might consider using focus groups to find out what employees, in general, would like to see included in the company's recognition program or process. Or, the team might use some method of written input—an idea box, E-mail, a clip-out included in the company newsletter, a survey (of everyone, of a sampling, of volunteers), or an input form sent out or made available through some other common communication medium. Employee input is necessary regardless of whether you already have a program in place or not. Sometimes what people would like and appreciate is not what the company has chosen to institute in the past. Even if employees originally liked the selected form of recognition, individual needs change as a result of workplace redesign and workforce maturation. Companies need to reassess constantly the design of their recognition processes and focus on continuous improvement.

Questions to consider when you begin to design (or redesign) your recognition process include the following:

Who will be on our design team? Why are these the best people to include?

What is the scope of the design effort?

What boundaries will be set?

What support will be provided to the team?

STEP 5: PILOTING/INTRODUCING THE PROGRAM

Even with careful attention to design, it is wise to take the time to *pilot* the recognition program or process. In some organizations, a true pilot can be done. This requires taking the time to institute a program or process in one area of the company, allowing a period of time (three to six months is common) of actual operation, and then evaluating the process in order to make decisions about whether the program is appropriate or whether it should be modified or dropped.

In other organizations, it is more appropriate to *phase in* a new program or process into one unit at a time based on a predetermined time line. Each successive implementation benefits from lessons learned in the preceding ones. Modifications can be made with each implementation. If you use the latter approach, begin implementation in representative areas of the organization (Remember, being asked to participate in a pilot or as an early participant can be a form of recognition in and of itself. However, this is only true when the request is appropriately handled.) A third alternative is to simply introduce the program or process to everyone at one time. This requires more management, especially in a large organization. If this alternative is selected, be sure to monitor carefully so that modifications can be introduced as needed. Continually ask: "What do you think? Are you taking advantage of the recognition? Why or why not?"

Regardless of what implementation process is appropriate to your organization and culture, allow time for people to understand, try out, and evaluate what is being introduced. Spend some time debriefing participants to find out what worked and what they would like to see handled differently. If selected properly, these individuals can also act as informal marketing spokespeople for the new program or process.

Consider the following:

- What will work in your organization—piloting, phased, or total implementation? Why?
- Are you prepared to provide an overview of what you intend to do and how it will be managed?

STEP 6: PREPARING FOR ROLLOUT

Recognition, whether company driven, team-based, or peer-to-peer, doesn't just happen. It represents a process, one that most employees have not experienced first-hand to any degree. Corporate programs are generally driven by managers, and the majority of companies do not have formalized team-based or peer-to-peer processes in place. For recognition to be truly effective and incorporated into the culture, organizations must adopt new ways of thinking. Reward systems need to belong to all employees, not just to managers. For this to happen, everyone in the organization will need to be *educated* to the new way of thinking.

Since culture change is driven top-down and through broad-based implementation, organizations must ensure

FIGURE 5–2
Key Elements of the Process

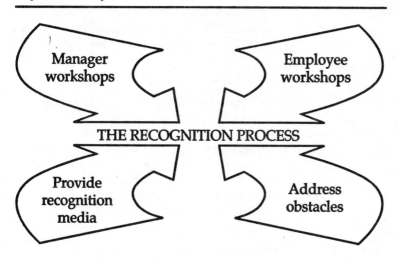

Manager workshops

Employee workshops

THE RECOGNITION PROCESS

Provide recognition media

Address obstacles

that everyone has the opportunity to understand the key elements of the recognition process so that it can operate effectively. Organizations can foster understanding, acceptance, and embracing of recognition by providing an environment in which this can occur.

Ultimately, each person decides for him or herself whether to take advantage of the corporate offering. In an environment that truly believes in and practices broad-based recognition, compensation systems will support the belief and employees will understand that failing to participate could negatively impact one's career. Corporations only take such a stand when they have gone through a careful planning process to understand and explain the strategic value of recognition to the corporation and to the individual. Recognition benefits the organization by benefiting the individual. The elements that make for a successful recognition process are shown in Figure 5–2.

The time spent in planning for the initial introduction of the process helps ensure that everyone hears the same corporate message. This communication effort will impact the success of recognition in the organization. The program or process being instituted needs to drive the form the communication takes. With management-driven programs, it can be quite short, often handled through an all-employee memo.

Example: A new company award was being initiated. The first ones were given out at an all-management meeting. At the end of the meeting, each attendee received an overview of the new award explaining what it was; why it was being introduced, and the "rules" for giving the recognition. About a week later, an all-employee memo was sent out. A few days later an article appeared in the company newspaper about the first awardees.

On the other hand, team-based and peer-to-peer recognition requires more extensive communication and training. These reflect a somewhat different concept than is found in most organizations and generally should be introduced through a workshop offered to all employees.

Example: The company introduced a peer-to-peer program. Understanding that most employees had never participated in such a program, a team of recognition trainers (interested individuals who formed the "R" Team) were recruited and they offered a one and a half hour workshop to everyone in the company.

Regardless of programs or processes selected, the organization must build in some mechanism to introduce current employees to any change in recognition-giving and to orient new employees to its recognition culture.

Workshops

Both managers and individual contributors need to *learn* about their role in the company's recognition program or process. Ask anyone about recognition and she will tell you that it is important. Ask the same individual exactly what she is doing personally to provide recognition to others in the organization, and her response will generally reveal that she isn't doing as much as she indicated was warranted when responding to the first question. Clearly, a gap exists. This is true for recognition programs that are management-driven and becomes an even greater issue for team-based and peer-to-peer-oriented approaches.

To overcome the gap, systems must be in place to oversee the implementation and maintenance of recognition systems. Organizations can use the Deming quality model of PDCA (plan, do, check, act) shown in Figure 5–3 as a way of ensuring that implementation is successful.

When planning your rollout, consider the amount of involvement each employee will have in the actual process. Recognize that the broader-based the involvement, the greater the need for training. What will you do at each stage of the cycle within your organization to ensure that the recognition you introduce will be implemented and maintained? Consider both the *what* and the *who* at each stage of the cycle.

Implementing management-driven models. Because of their lack of exposure to, and training in, the areas of rewards and recognition, most managers do not sufficiently value or understand the power of recognition to support it as they should for it to be successful. Managers often lack the skills required in giving recognition, which reduces their ability to practice and model recognition for the rest of the organization. A manager's workshop will address these shortfalls and demonstrate an organization's commitment to recognition. In organizations where

FIGURE 5–3
Recognition PDCA Cycle

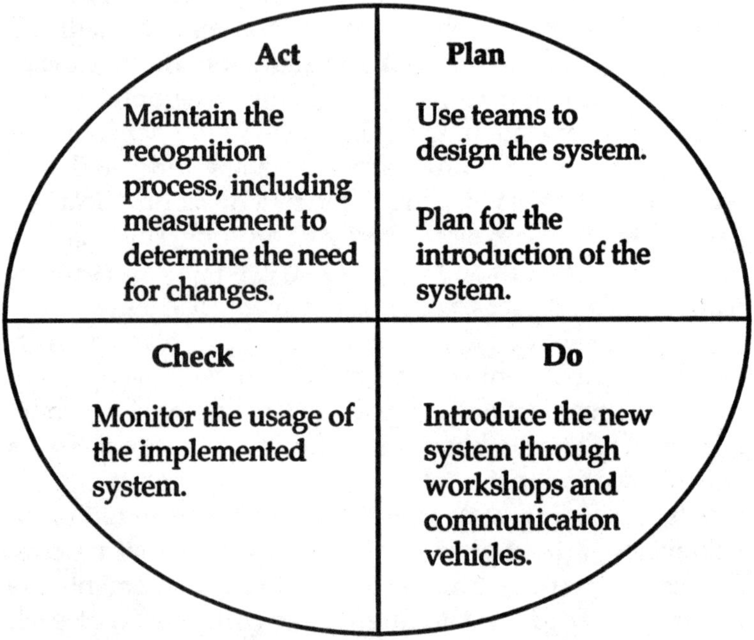

Act	Plan
Maintain the recognition process, including measurement to determine the need for changes.	Use teams to design the system. Plan for the introduction of the system.
Check	**Do**
Monitor the usage of the implemented system.	Introduce the new system through workshops and communication vehicles.

recognition is a strategy, that is, when someone has taken time to map out employee groups against the company vision and philosophy, workshops can become a tool. They can ensure that all managers and leaders understand the value of recognition to the organization and take action that furthers the corporate recognition strategy.

Corporate programs tend to be management-focused and generally minimize employee involvement. Thus, for these programs, employee orientation is often minimal. A brochure available to all employees can explain the programs that are in place. If employees are able to nominate others for recognition, the process for doing so must be spelled out. Requisite forms need to be either generally provided or how to get them needs to be clearly spelled out. Materials also must be easy to access. Ideally employees can get the information and materials they need through a resource *outside* and in addition to the manager. You shouldn't cut the manager out of the cycle, but you also shouldn't rely totally on this one resource. The dual resource allows employees a degree of confidentiality if they so desire. It also can compensate for managers who aren't supportive of the process. If your program represents a completely new concept within the organization, you should plan to have some type of broad-based introduction. Some ways to introduce a management-driven program include the following:

- Managers discussing the program at their unit meetings.
- Providing scripts for those who will be sharing the new program or process so that all employees will hear the same message.
- Selecting (through self-appointment or identification) individuals who can present a common message about the new program or process to team meetings.
- Including information on the program or process and listing early awardees in the company news media.
- Making recognition a regular feature of each communication video (if your company has one). This can be especially powerful if your organization sends videos to employees at home because significant others can learn of recognition within the organization.
- Holding an all-employee rally.
- Including an information piece about recognition in the company communications vehicle. This can become a teaching or modeling tool.
- Sending out a companywide communication—and don't forget to consider using electronic means, such as E-mail and shared LANS.

- Putting up banners or other forms of publicity throughout the organization to make the new program or process visible.

Choose the means of introduction that will work best in your environment. The key is to make sure that everyone hears about the program in a timely manner and in the same way. Don't select a vehicle for informing that relies on solely managers to share at their discretion. Too many will be hesitant to share information that they might not be comfortable with. Your goal is to ensure that managers are not in a position to discount the importance of recognition and thus prevent the initiative's success. Elements that must be included in the information dissemination process include the following:

- Why use the program or process—tie it to company philosophy or vision.
- What role do managers and nonmanagerial employees play?
- Details—what can be given, how it is given, who does the giving, when it is done, where giving is done.

Implementing and maintaining team-based and peer-involvement models. By their nature, these models cut across the organization and target high levels of involvement. They generally reflect processes that will encourage employees to observe what is going on in the workplace and to acknowledge what they see by directly rewarding others. Taking the initiative to share information about the achievement of others relies on skills that most people have not regularly practiced in their jobs. To implement these models, attention must be given to developing the required recognition-giving and communication skills in employees. They need the opportunity to practice the skills in a safe environment. Experience suggests that this is best accomplished in a workshop setting. This ensures the following:

- Everyone hears the same message.
- The message is shared in a timely manner.
- It is a positive message that encourages people to recognize each other's work.
- Everyone has the opportunity to try out, or at minimum, to see what good recognition-giving looks like.

Both a *cascade* (one level of the organization learns and then trains the level beneath it) and a *training team* or *cadre model* (a team that is trained with the intent to do all the training or to train others to train in other parts of the organization) are effective methods of sharing the information. Each model will disseminate the necessary knowledge throughout the organization and at the same time position key individuals or managers in the role of educator. Remember, key people must be actively involved for recognition to be effective—these models encourage active participation. Some characteristics that you would want in those selected as instructors include the following:

- Good teaching skills (these are not the same as presentation skills).
- High degree of credibility in the organization.
- Demonstrated belief in recognition and its value. These are best supported by personal "war stories" of how reward and recognition helped the individual.
- An attitude of fun that needs to permeate any team-based or peer-to-peer process for it to be embraced by employees.

Developing recognition-giving skills. In addition to the train-the-trainer sessions, two other types of workshops should be considered: manager sessions and employee sessions. In a hierarchical organization the traditional manager/employee separation can dictate what is covered in each session. In a self-directed team environment, everyone should participate in a "leader" session.

A manager session should consist of a recognition overview that reviews reward and recognition in general, team-based and peer-to-peer recognition specifically, and the manager's role in the process. The goals of this workshop include the following:

- To help managers understand and appreciate the value of recognition as a motivational tool.
- To encourage them to recognize and address any personal views or biases they may hold regarding recognition and its place within their organization.
- In a team-based organization, to address how the "new" leader/manager or coach can support recognition.

A basic influence on team success is effective reward and recognition systems that support the new, desired team behaviors. In the new organization, managers will no longer drive recognition. Instead, they become advisers whose roles are to provide guidance so that teams adopt rewards that are in line with the organization's guidelines. The leader will need to help kick off, reinforce, and maintain reward and recognition in the new team-based environment.

Manager workshops should be held before employee sessions. If trainers have not yet been identified, these workshops can help identify future potential trainers. A half-day session can suffice to present the material identified in Table 5–1, as appropriate for manager workshops.

TABLE 5–1
Suggested Workshop Content

Topic	Manager's and Team Leader Workshop	Employee Workshop
Recognition as a strategy—corporate and personal	X	
What is peer-to-peer recognition?	X	X
Gap analysis—where we are versus where we want to be	X	
Manager's role in recognition	X	
Role and responsibility of individual employees in a peer-to-peer recognition environment	X	X
Team recognition systems—what to include, how to do it effectively, why it is important to team success	X	X
Role and responsibility of the leader/advisor in the team-based organization	X	X
An organization assessment—who are we, what kinds of recognition will work here, how can we accommodate our diversity	X	X
Self-assessment—personal attitudes around recognition (includes personal gap analysis)	X	X
Recognition tools—what is available within the organization	X	X
Ideas for low- or no-cost recognition that individuals can use with or without company support	X	X
Rightness of specific recognition ideas	X	X
Obstacles and pitfalls—corporate and personal	X	X
Action planning	X	X

You should also build time for practice into the sessions. This is important because most managers have not been trained in how to give informal recognition and need the opportunity to try out new behavior in a safe environment. (This is true even though they will tell you they don't need the practice.)

Employee sessions focus more on helping individuals to understand how recognition can benefit the work group: what's in it for each person, for the team, and for the organization as a whole. Individual contributors need to learn about the recognition process and the company tools that are available to them. They also need to learn *how* to get involved as both givers and receivers of recognition. This is especially important in environments that have not provided much recognition in the past. Employees will also benefit if you include structured practice sessions with immediate feedback built into the process (even better if on-the-job reinforcement by the manager/leader is also planned for).

Team-based training can be provided to teams using a Just-In-Time (JIT) approach. As soon as a team is ready to deal with how they will recognize and reward each other's contributions, training needs to be available. Although recognition is not the first item that newly formed teams address, most *are* interested in thinking about how they reward and recognize contributions fairly early in the team's life cycle. Recognition is not the same as performance management, which is something that should be addressed later when the team is more mature.

If the manager is the facilitator for the employee sessions, she will be positioned to play a more active role with the team back on the job. The managers' participation will help employees understand that management does in fact actively encourage recognition and support the process. Workshops can be two to four hours in duration, depending upon the culture and environment previously in place. The greater the gap between the new and old cultures, the longer the sessions will need to be. If you are making massive culture shifts, consider offering the workshop content through a series of one-hour sessions spread out over time. Employees can practice specific types of recognition and will have opportunity for feedback about how they are performing. Plan to allow time for questions and answers at these sessions, and encourage the sharing of success stories among participants. Suggested content for the employee workshops are detailed in Table 5–1.

Consider the following items as you prepare for your roll out of reward and recognition systems in your organization:

Which model will work in your organization?

What type of workshops will you provide?

Who will do the training, and who will be included?

What content topics are appropriate for your organization?

STEP 7: PLANNING FOR INFRASTRUCTURE SUPPORT

The planning process must account for the allocation of resources and budget to recognition. What is going to be done by whom, when and how, and at what cost? Examples of needed support include the following:

Allowing people time to give recognition to each other.

Providing the materials required for no-cost giving.

Modeling the desired behaviors.

Having vehicles in place to positively acknowledge those who give recognition.

Infrastructure support is especially important in team-based and peer-to-peer recognition processes. Unless the support is in place, recognition becomes *verbiage*. One important function of the awareness workshops is to help individuals understand the resources (time, materials, human) that constitute the recognition process. Because it doesn't just *happen*, commitment requires actively making sure that the necessary resources are in place so that people can and will participate.

Another key is to provide required resources. If you are supporting no-or low-cost recognition, some actions you might consider include:

- At least initially, make sure that supplies are in place to allow people to give the recognition.
- Purchase a computer program package that generates posters, banners, notes, certificates, and so forth. Load it onto a dedicated PC that employees can easily access.
- See that printers and copiers are readily available so that people can take advantage.
- Provide a kiosk(s) where employees can get and use supplies as needed.

Plan ahead for the new world of local area networks (LAN's) and wide area networks (WAN's) and their influence on your organization's support programs. Should you consider putting recognition software onto the network? This implies a willingness to allow employees much greater, unsupervised access to recognition media. Are you ready for this? Your answer makes a statement about your support for recognition and your trust in employees' ability to use provided resources wisely.

What are you doing to plan for infrastructure support? One thing you might consider is to write a brief plan outlining the infrastructure support you intend to institute and maintain. Be sure to address the future in your plan.

Example: In one organization the training department acquired one older-model PC for making certificates and banners. This was feasible because the organization was moving to windows technology and the older models had been depreciated and were now excess inventory. Many of the "award-type" programs are DOS-based and don't require substantial memory.

STEP 8: EVALUATING AND PLANNING FOR PROCESS IMPROVEMENT

People and conditions change, so it makes sense to build into your recognition system a way to evaluate the process. This will help you make changes as they are needed. Even if the initial system was excellent and well-received, today's organization changes so quickly that programs instituted in the 80s or earlier won't necessarily continue to be appropriate—analogous to a quality initiative's emphasis on continuous improvement. Recognize that the "programs" that you institute will have much shorter lives than do your "processes" or "systems." Plan to evaluate your programs at three-to-six-month intervals. The following techniques can help you determine how appropriate your program or process is:

• Provide evaluation forms for all employees on a periodic basis. The more well-received and used the process, the less frequently you need to evaluate. At a minimum, plan for some type of evaluation at least every two years to ensure continued effectiveness.

• Gather feedback from the recipients of rewards (these are the customers). Ask them what they think of your program or process. Do this anonymously or through a third party, because people are often hesitant to share negative thoughts, especially when they have been given a *company* honor.

• Bring together focus groups to talk about how people would like to be recognized. The output of the session will be a wish list for the future, not a compendium of what is available today or a "finger-pointing" list. The discrepancies that surface between what is desired and what exists inform you about the appropriateness of current programs and processes. They also provide you with direction for the future.

• Monitor usage: Is a cross-section of employees actually submitting names for recognition? Which of the in-place vehicles are people using? Look for numbers and for trends.

Be sure you share the results of what you learn about your program or process. Do this on a broad base. If change is warranted, involve people from throughout the organization. In today's fast-changing world, an attitude of continuous improvement is required. Be wary of the program or process that continues to be *perfect*—continuous perfection is generally not a real condition but a sign of some underlying problem (apathy, fear, or lack of knowledge are potential problems).

The following questions can help you plan for evaluation and continuous process improvement:

Are you knowledgeable enough about recognition and your organization's needs to outline your plan to evaluate your recognition program or process?

Who will do what?

How will it be done? At what frequency?

STEP 9: PROVIDING FOR ONGOING SUPPORT OF IN-PLACE SYSTEMS

Maintenance (how we keep it alive) of any instituted process is probably the most difficult piece and is one that is best planned for in advance. Even good programs and

> The company had a bulletin board of thank-you letters and memos. Employees were encouraged to post copies of any correspondence they sent to co-workers commending their contribution. To remind people of the board the background paper was changed monthly—bright colors were always used to catch the eye of those passing by. People regularly stopped to read the posted items. Periodically a banner was posted over the bulletin board to, again, draw attention to the board and its contents. Since the focus was "thank you's", the sponsor of the board passed out treats periodically to remind people to give a written thank you to their peers.

processes can suffer from inertia over time. It is not enough to design and introduce a good program; it is also necessary to plan for ways to see that people are constantly reminded of the recognition systems that are available.

For most people recognition is something that must be actively thought about because it is not a part of normal behavior. In few environments do people continually, spontaneously recognize each others' contributions. More commonly, there is a well-received and participated-in introductory period, followed by dwindling interest. This is especially evident when people have had to go through workshops or training to learn the importance of recognition and to receive help with the process, because they have not yet made it a part of ingrained behavior.

Behavior generally falls into one of four categories, shown in Figure 5–4. These also represent the sequence in which an individual becomes aware of and develops skills in a new area.

Training gets people to Stage III of Figure 5–4; maintenance planning gets individuals to Stage IV. Any organization committed to recognition must understand this

FIGURE 5–4
Stages of Skill Development

	Low Level of Conscious Thinking	High Level of Conscious Thinking
Low Productivity	**STAGE I** The individual doesn't know about a better/ different way of operating. This is a state of uneducated oblivion.	**STAGE II** The individual becomes aware of a better/ different way of operating and is now aware of her or his lack of skill. This *is* a state of educated incompetence.
High Productivity	**STAGE IV** The individual, through practice, has developed a high degree of skill and is considered to be proficient. This eventually reaches a state of unconscious competence.	**STAGE III** The individual learns how to do the better/ different way but is still unsophisticated in practicing the behavior. This is a state of emerging competence.

tendency to backslide into old habits and build in ways of countering it. Some techniques that might be considered include the following:

• Talk about the process on a regular basis—talk about what is being done and verbally reference any modeling that is going on. Be sure to build in a strategy that will ensure that employees hear about recognition from the organization's models and champions.

• Provide incentives for people to get involved. Be sure to refer to those who participate in company programs. You might do this by acknowledging people who are recommending or recognizing others or by giving monetary rewards to those who are exemplary in their recognition of others.

• Provide ongoing education about recognition: the process, the benefits, how-tos. Once is not enough. People must hear repeatedly about how to give recognition. Build a curriculum that includes information about recognition within other training programs or provides mini-sessions to introduce or reinforce specific points about rewards and recognition.

• Make it fun. Use the carrot rather than the stick as a way of getting people involved.

As you get ready to plan for ongoing support systems, consider the following questions:

What can you do to maintain the recognition system in your organization?

What specifically needs to be done?

How will it be done?

Who will be responsible for the maintenance?

A company wanted to reinforce good reward and recognition behavior in employees. Approximately three months after initial training, a Maintenance and Motivation (M&M) program was introduced. Everyone got a bag of M&Ms at the kick-off. Each employee was also given a coupon book to identify positive reward and recognition behavior (who, what). Anyone receiving five coupons in a month was invited to a barbeque held during lunch, with the management staff doing the cooking. This provided a high-involvement way of saying thank you, and everyone had fun. (Five may seem like a lot, but remember that saying thank you is a form of recognition and also needs to be encouraged and reinforced.)

The steps detailed above will provide the framework for designing, implementing, and maintaining an effective recognition process within your organization.

Use the guide in Table 5–2 as a reminder to see that you complete each step required to establish a recognition system. Short-circuiting steps because of workplace constraints will reduce the effectiveness of the system you implement.

Keeping a program or process alive takes energy; understand this before you get involved. Taking the initial step and then dropping the effort because of lack of follow-through will make employees cynical about the supposed culture and vision or philosophy of the organization around recognition. It will also make it doubly hard to attempt to institute a recognition culture in the future.

Once you have a plan in place, take some time to guard against the common pitfalls to recognition, reviewed in Chapter 6.

TABLE 5-2
Steps to Establishing a Recognition System Planning Guide

Step	Currently Doing— Yes/No?	Plan to Do in the Near Future— Yes/No?	How Will It Look When the Step Has Been Implemented within Your Organization?	Who Will Be Responsible?	By When?
Step 1: Establishing the foundation for recognition in the organization					
Step 2: Selecting the champion for the process					
Step 3: Deciding what we shall include in our process					
Step 4: Establishing a design team					
Step 5: Plotting the program					
Step 6: Preparing for rollout					
Step 7: Planning for infrastructure support					
Step 8: Evaluating and planning for process improvement					
Step 9: Providing for ongoing support					

An organization moving to a team-based environment spent some time with representatives from each work unit to identify ways to get everyone involved in the recognition process. The decision was that a role model, while necessary, wasn't enough. The representatives recognized that employees differed in their comfort and skill in giving recognition. As a consequence, workshops to teach people how to give recognition were initiated, and periodic refresher workshops were planned for.

As a result, employees in this organization own the recognition system. A cross-functional team (including managers and individual contributors) is responsible for the recognition process within the organization. The team designed the program, drove its implementation, and continues to monitor it. Focus groups are periodically assembled to evaluate the appropriateness of the process, and changes to improve the system are made based on employee input. Over time many new no/low-cost options have been added or removed at the request of individuals on the teams. Because employees own the process, they like their system. Measures of usage indicate that the majority of employees regularly make use of its vehicles. As might be expected with such a dynamic process, the current system looks different from the one originally instituted

Chapter 6

Pitfalls to Watch Out For

Successful implementation is more than introducing a reward and recognition program or process and providing the resources to support it. The obstacles to recognition must be identified and addressed at a conscious level: the barriers are first identified and solutions are then developed to deal with them within the organization or team (or internally if at a personal level). Commonly met obstacles and pitfalls to recognition, along with potential solutions that might be considered to address them, are discussed in this chapter. The pitfalls are categorized by those felt at a corporate level and those that teams and individuals must deal with.

PITFALLS RELATED TO PROGRAM DESIGN ISSUES

The following pitfalls relate to design and are ones that will surface early in the developmental process.

By the Corporation, For the Corporation

A key to successful recognition is to have all involved parties participate in the design of the system. If the corporation, relying on its Human Resource or Quality function,

---

A Danger

Telling people they will be responsible for the design of the system and then not using or incorporating the recommendations they provide.

---

designs the program in a vacuum or considers only the senior management team as the customer, the program will not be successful. The company will have a "paper" program, one that may receive the approval of senior officers but that employees will not buy into.

Potential solution. Have a design team that represents a cross section of company employees. Make it the responsibility of this group to determine what types of recognition will be appropriate. Include individuals from various organizational levels and units to allow for the inclusion of ideas that reflect reward and recognition needs of all employees. Do this even though final buy-off of the plan must be by the senior managers. As long as employees understand that they are to provide only input into the process, to suggest the best design, and are not to make the final decision as to the program selected, they will be more likely to accept their assigned role up front and to live with the final design at the back end.

Slanted to One Segment of the Corporation (Either in Giving or Receiving)

Sometimes companies with the best of intentions set up a recognition program that targets particular employee groups. For example, a program might recognize big, high-risk contributors but do nothing for the consistent but not highly visible employees (who constitute approximately 80 percent of most workforces). Or, a program might allow only managers above a certain level to give input about who should be recognized, thus limiting recognition to those individuals the management group happens to know personally.

Potential solution.   Create a matrix of all employee groups within the company. Use this to determine accessibility to and inclusion in the recognition process for each group. Exclusions will be very visible; thus, strategies can be developed to ensure that all groups are included. A sample matrix is shown in Table 6–1.

No Attention to Comprehensive Implementation Planning

Effectively implemented recognition takes a great deal of planning. Attention must be given to how to introduce the program so everyone will participate.

Potential solution.   Take time during the initial design stage to think through how the plan will be introduced to each employee group within the company. Identify potential and probable obstacles that will need to be addressed. Some common ones that most organizations face include:

- Ensuring that all employees receive unbiased information about the program or process—this means presenting information in a positive way and preventing managers who are negative about recognition from destroying it within their work areas based on the way it is introduced.

TABLE 6-1
Establishing Involvement in the Recognition Process

Role in Program/Process	Employee Groups				
	Managers	*Individual Contributors*	*Team Units*	*Exempt Staff*	*Nonexempt Staff*
Able to recommend to others that recognition be given					
Are empowered to initiate the process but not to follow through to final awarding					
Are empowered to do the physical giving of the recognition					
Can receive recognition that is initiated by management					
Can receive recognition from the team					
Can receive recognition from peers					
Have easy and direct access to the structured company recognition program as initiators of recognition					
Are eligible to and have a high degree of probability of receiving recognition through the structured company program					

- Enlisting individuals in positions of power. You will need a champion—pick a person in the organization who is visible and highly regarded, one who will take ownership of the process. *All* leaders/managers need to model the desired recognition behaviors. Organizations must take the necessary steps to prevent recognition from becoming a "Do as I say, not as I do" program. This is a sure-fire *killer* of any system put in place.
- Pretesting and announcing plans to get recognition materials out within the organization.

No Attention to the Mechanics that Support Recognition in the Organization

Telling everyone about recognition and then not providing continuing support is dealing only with the first half the process. It is also important to see that necessary supplies, whether they be recommendation forms or actual recognition media, are readily available.

Potential solution. Be sure to think through what will be needed and build in a budget and people to make sure that the supports that will keep the process or program alive are in place.

If there are to be *keepers* of the material, be sure they understand the procedures and have the necessary supplies. Don't put these individuals in the position of not knowing any more than the rest of the organization. It is helpful to position the keeper close to the audience—don't make people walk to an uncomfortable spot to get the needed supplies—for example, don't have the person who holds the recognition materials sit in the executive, mahogany row.

Recognize that simply putting a plan together on paper does not guarantee that it will work. Find some low-keyed and low-risk area and do some piloting to make sure the implementation plan actually works as it was designed.

Not Addressing Strategic Aspects of Recognition

Recognition can be a strategic tool in managing employee satisfaction within the corporation and in motivating people to greater levels of achievement. To be strategic, recognition must be thought through, and it must be long-term in its focus. The focus is on recognition as a *process* (a way of thinking and behaving) rather than as just a program.

Potential solution.   Consciously address recognition as a strategy. The designers of a recognition process must have a vision of how it will fit in and enhance the corporate vision. As plans are developed, the vision can become the litmus test for strategic design issues. Planning ahead and knowing where the organization needs to be in two to five years will enable recognition to support and enhance overall business plans. Be sure to address the following elements in your planning process:

- What is the corporate vision?
- How can recognition help the organization achieve its corporate vision?
- What would a complementary recognition vision be?
- What are the critical success factors that will influence the achievement of this vision?
- What steps need to be taken to address these factors?
- Can the value added of recognition be identified, quantified, and measured?

When the organization migrates to work teams, recognition takes on a more significant role and must be included in the strategic HR or Quality planning process. Generally, new forms of reward and recognition systems are needed in an environment where individuals take more control of the operations of their work unit. There tends to be greater emphasis placed on low or no-cost forms of recognition in such environments because they are more easily controlled by individual contributors and teams.

PITFALLS RELATED TO CORPORATE CULTURE ISSUES

Culture drives and controls the success of any recognition system an organization might implement. It may be "unspoken," but culture is loud and clear in its ability to determine the success of any reward and recognition program or process. Therefore, potential cultural pitfalls must be identified and dealt with. The following describes some of the issues that arise in organizations that are moving to a recognition-valuing culture and identifies potential solutions to these issues. As you read through these pitfalls, think in terms of your own organization's culture: evaluate which ones might impact your ability to institute a reward and recognition system in your company.

"But Will They Buy It?" Issues

What works in one organization will not necessarily work in another. Recognition systems must match the culture into which they are being adopted. Benchmarking is important, however an organization cannot simply see a program or process being used in another place and import it because it is successful in the original environment. It is critical that program designers look to the people who staff their particular organization and ask, What are they like? Specific career fields tend to attract different types of individuals. For example, a recognition that would work well with a team of sales people would quite likely not be effective with a group of information systems programmers. The former would probably like spontaneous, visible, showy, heavily interactive recognition, while the latter would quite likely prefer personal, planned, private recognition. Using the wrong form of recognition can be worse than not giving any at all.

Potential solutions. First don't try to carbon copy the rewards and recognition of another organization, no matter how well they work in that environment. You will need to begin by spending some time assessing your own culture and the individuals who work in the organization. Try piloting new ideas to see how they are accepted. Get people involved in deciding how recognition might be given within the organization. Bring in several diverse model programs as a way of helping a group decide what will work. Picking and choosing and building your own will increase the likelihood of success.

The Recognition Process Is Driven Top-Down but Must Be Owned at All Levels of the Organization

Ownership includes determining what is given, how it is given, how it is supported. Managers sometimes assume a parental attitude that says or implies, "I will *take care of* my people, establish a good recognition *program for them,* make sure everything is in place for it to *work for them,* and then *remove myself* from it." Notice the italicized words. They reflect both a parenting attitude and a separation of the people who *own* the program from those who *use* it. When either or both of these happen, people within the organization are much less likely to use or buy into the process.

Potential solutions. The goal is to make sure that everyone on the management team understands that recognition must be owned by the entire organization. The *benevolent dictator* approach does not work in today's team-oriented, flattened corporation. Organizations can't provide one-flavor recognition exclusively for management and another one exclusively for peer-to-peer processes. The need for team-based recognition adds an additional dimension. Recognition boundaries must be set at the senior management level, but teams that are empowered and self-directed will take the lead in driving the actual recognition system. While what is given will naturally vary according to the target audience of a program, a feeling of ownership of the system at large exists in the corporation.

The planning process must ensure that system pieces dovetail and that rewards and recognition do not appear to be segmented or stratified. Questions that might be asked to assure cohesiveness of the system include the following:

- Who uses this program element?
- Could people construe what is available to different groups in the organization as more or less valuable, based on who can access the recognition media?
- What would make you say, "People in our organization own the recognition program or process in place here?" Be specific in your explanation.

The training of managers can ensure that they know how best to support the organization's system. This includes how to give and get the recognition, how to evaluate the attitude about recognition, and how to support it. Training employees encourages them to take an active role in the process—this is a requisite to ownership and is especially important in a team-based environment.

Not Looking at Culture First in Order to Match Recognition with What Works in the Culture

Knowing your own organization is a starting point for recognition. There can be a difference between what we *think* our culture should be and what it really is. Before developing any recognition, it is important to take the time to establish what the corporate culture really is. This information will ensure that you are able to design processes that will be meaningful to employees who actually work in the organization. Some cultures foster heavy people involvement and celebration; others are more reserved and low-keyed. It is not an issue of one being better than another; it is instead an issue of knowing what will work in your environment—match what the culture will buy into with what is offered.

Potential solution.   Before you plan your process or program, spend some time looking at your own culture. Do a formal needs assessment if necessary. Once you have profiled what good recognition looks like in your culture (i.e., the key elements that must be included and how they should be accommodated), you will be better positioned to develop processes that will succeed.

Some culture elements that you might consider include the following:

• Think of the typical employee. Where on the introvert/extrovert scale would you place that person? What about the typical team? Where would you place your CEO? Where would you place the management team as a whole?

Completely introverted   Extremely extroverted

▲_____▲_____▲

• What type of celebrations do you currently have in your organization and how accepted have they been? Think about who initiates the celebrations and who participates in them.

Very spontaneous,
lots of informality
and laughter

Formal, held at
regular intervals.

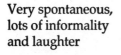

• How easy is it to cross job-grade levels for recognition giving within your organization? Do senior managers make themselves visible and available to all employees? Are there clear boundaries within which one can initiate recognition interaction?

Anyone can recognize
anyone. We have a
completely open-
door approach.

The boxes of our
organization chart
are very rigidly
adhered to and these
dictate who can
recognize whom.

Not Recognizing the Pull of the "Old" Culture

Once the hoopla is over, people need to be reminded regularly of recognition—this is what maintenance is all about. Methods of ensuring that whatever is implemented continues to exist must also be included. This requires an ongoing dedication and involvement on the part of key players. Maintenance is the piece that is often not attended to but that ultimately determines the success of the initial implementation effort. As mentioned earlier, a general rule for institutionalizing any new behavior is that it takes approximately 20 tries to make a behavior one's own. If the organization is to make recognition its own, key players must be ready to do a great deal of modeling and reinforcement of the desired behavior. The best support includes performance and verbalization, because these provide a double reinforcement.

An important element to consider when a program is introduced is to take into account how people react to what is "new."

25%	Immediately support a new initiative
50%	Take a wait-and-see attitude, remain neutral, observing activity at both ends of the scale
25%	Reject the initiative immediately, are not adverse to sabotaging and actively countering the initiative

Approximately 50 percent of employees react neutrally to new things that are brought in. How you deal with this group and find ways to move them to the support side will impact the success of your initiative. Since you know the statistics, focus on ways to motivate employees to get involved in the new recognition system in a positive way.

Maintenance takes effort. Too often, key players who are willing to do the initial work to introduce something they believe in slack off in their reinforcement efforts over time because of other corporate pressures. The verbal enthusiasm may continue to be there, but the ongoing, daily support simply dies out over time. Often this happens because of the energy required to keep the recognition process going. To keep the energy level high, there is a need to constantly bring in new ideas. Make sure there is a structured plan in place to regularly introduce new ways for people to recognize one another.

Potential solution. Spend time up front talking about and planning for the energy it takes to maintain recognition systems. Don't rely on one individual to keep things going; institute a "team" to help with the process. Have a backlog of "new" ideas to reinforce the recognition systems. Make sure you pick ones that can be introduced on a regular basis without too much effort.

PITFALLS FACING THE TEAM AND/OR INDIVIDUAL EMPLOYEE

Ultimately it is the people in the organization who determine the success of any recognition process that is introduced. It is important that the design and implementation processes are built around a clearly profiled target population and that these account for human reaction to anything new. Think about and plan for how people generally react to changes in the organization and how individuals can best be approached with new ideas.

Recognition is no different from any other process that is newly instituted or changed: you can expect people to react and resist. A trap is to forget about the typical human reaction to change and bring in new recognition programs or processes too quickly and in too rapid succession. When each new idea is touted as the best way to make things better in the organization, an outfall is that people become inundated with too much change, and they become skeptical of anything new. That is, they move from the earlier discussed neutral camp to the negative camp. This is true even though a proposed reward or recognition might be *good* for the individuals and for the company. Breaking down negative views takes time and a great deal of energy. It is simpler to take a proactive approach and focus on demonstrating the benefits of the new" to everyone and thus help move the 50 percent of the wait-and-see people in the direction you wish. When this is not done, employees are more likely to succumb to the potential human pitfalls. Some of the more common pitfalls are discussed below.

People Feel Silly Giving Recognition

Do any of the following typify the situation in your organization?

Giving recognition has not always been allowed or encouraged.

Recognizing others has always been a management prerogative.

Recognition is something that is formal and serious.

If you agreed with any of these statements, understand that empowering individuals to recognize one another's contributions directly and immediately will be uncomfortable, both for managers and for individual contributors. Acknowledge that there is a degree of risk taking involved when someone recognizes another's contribution for the first time.

Potential solution.   Consider the comfort zone of the giver. Things that are outside the zone will be avoided by many in the early stages of implementing any recognition program. Filling out a *request for recognition* is fairly safe and would be more palatable to people unfamiliar with recognition than would be making a blue ribbon, taking someone a cup of coffee, or giving a *spoonful of kisses* (a plastic spoon with a few Hershey's Kisses wrapped in cellophane). A major emphasis of the manager and individual contributor workshops must address and cope with these normal human reactions to new forms of giving. If you are providing materials for low or no-cost recognition, think of the comfort zone of employees and provide appropriate supplies. Starting out with a computer program to let people make banners and certificates of appreciation is a safe beginning point because it is less personal and is easy to do.

No One Is Willing to Take Responsibility for the Process

A new process becomes *just another program* unless individuals are motivated to take ownership and get involved.

Potential solution. Initially identify and recruit a respected individual or group of interested people who believe in recognition—corporate, team-based, and peer-to-peer. This person or group can champion the value of and fun in all types of recognition and recruit others into the process. Broad-based ownership is critical to the success of recognition. Early proponents must understand paradigm shifts and be able to continue *selling* the value of the recognition process in spite of resistance (passive primarily) that is normal and predictable.

KISS

The acronym KISS (Keep It Short and Simple) is most appropriate for effective recognition, whether corporate, team-based, or peer-to-peer. It supports the goal of the recognition process, which is to encourage individuals to acknowledge regularly one another's contributions and to do so in the simplest way possible.

Potential solution. People are more likely to get involved in recognition if the process is simple and quick. One measure is the speed with which the system can be explained to employees. A program that takes a half day to explain will probably not be used; one that people can understand and see the value of in 30 minutes or less will be more likely to be used. Understand that to establish a *simple* program will take a great deal of planning and preparation.

Accepting and Embracing Humor

We need to take our jobs seriously and ourselves lightly.
Most organizations and the people within don't *live*
this concept, however. Recognition fosters a lighter attitude, especially through its team-based and peer-to-peer
expressions.

Potential solution. For a lighter attitude to be accepted, management must model the desired attitudes.
Employees will be much more willing to partake if they
see key people in the organization setting the light tone
necessary for peer recognition to work effectively. You may
have to provide a structure or script at first to help set the
humorous tone you seek. Providing early supports will encourage people to try the light approach.

Accommodating Human Diversity

Today's workplace is characterized by diversity. Diversity
of race and ethnicity, of personality, of cultural norms, of
lifestyles, and of work experiences and values are a few
of the ways people who come together in the workplace
are different. It is important to address and accommodate
this diversity when giving recognition. The saying, "Different strokes for different folks," is most appropriate. As
you plan for recognition, spend some time addressing the
issue of what kinds of recognition are most appropriate
for your particular organization, based on the people who
populate it.

Some common questions that surface as you begin to
think about the diversity in your organization include: Is
formal correct? Must or should recognition be rolled down
and controlled from above? Is team-based and peer-to-peer
appropriate? Is this a food culture, a "make something" culture, a banner/certificate culture? And, how *light* can we be?

Potential solution. There is a broad range of acceptable recognition behavior. It is important that employees understand the behavior boundaries in their organization. Setting boundaries is the key to empowerment when it comes to recognition. Individuals are much more likely to get involved when they are free to access a variety of company and team/peer-controlled vehicles that have been designed to match the organization's diverse population and still be within acceptable company behavior limits. These boundaries can be explained through memos, war stories, training, and modeling.

Clearly defining boundaries also prevents anyone from being "set up" because they chose a form of recognition inappropriate to the environment, which can happen when no limits are set.

Another option is to take advantage of the workshops on cultural diversity that many organizations are offering employees. It would be most appropriate to add a unit on "recognition in a diverse workplace" as part of any session that is held. If this is not feasible, the topic could be included as part of recognition training.

Time

An organization must make it "O.K." to take the time to give recognition. This is especially true for team-based and peer-to-peer recognition. Approval is demonstrated by allowing *time* for such activity. What happens when the message sent is: "Sure, it's okay to give the recognition, but do it all on your own time. Don't take any of the workday for the recognition process." Guess how many people will get involved! Employees frequently identify time issues when they are asked why they feel that management does not support a new process (regardless of what it is).

Potential solution. The workshops held for managers and individual contributors can address the time issue from both sides. Managers need to allow and encourage the giving of recognition on company time, including the time to get the reward ready. Employees also need to recognize that this is a new process and that it is their responsibility to see that they do not abuse the right to use this new process on company time. It can help to set initial guidelines for time as long as everyone understands that these are just guidelines and not time mandates.

Companies as well as employees must recognize that obstacles will surface. An effective strategy will identify potential pitfalls before they are encountered. Plans to deal with probable and potential obstacles based on a knowledge of the organization, its culture, and its employee population can be developed ahead of time to ensure as smooth an implementation as possible. Table 6–1 can help you identify pitfalls that might affect implementation within your organization and can help you develop a road map to navigate around them. Go back through the pitfalls described in this chapter and identify two or three that you feel might impact the rewards and recognition system in your organization. Use the matrix to guide your development of an action plan to deal with those issues that are pertinent to you, your team, and your organization. Consider this an ongoing planning process. Once you have completed an action, develop a new one to pursue.

Once you are ready to implement your program, you will need to come up with appropriate rewards and recognition for your organization. The lists provided in Chapter 7 can help you with this identification process. Remember to involve all the recognition system customers (both givers and receivers) in the planning process.

TABLE 6–1
Action Planning Guide to Deal with Pitfalls

Issue	Potential Impact		Action Plans			
	High	Low	What Will Be Done	People Involved	Critical Success Factors	By When

Chapter 7

Recognition Ideas

This chapter includes lists of recognition ideas that work. They have been collected during the past several years from diverse groups working in many organizations, in different occupations, in different geographic locations, and at various levels of responsibility within their organizations. We gathered the ideas by asking audiences, "What was your favorite, most memorable recognition (especially low or no-cost) that you have given, received, or heard about?"

As you develop your own recognition programs and processes, you might consider periodically asking individuals in your organization what works for them and adding these to your initial lists. Remember the Platinum Rule: "Do unto others as they would like to be done unto." Until you find out what types of recognition are meaningful to the people being recognized, your efforts will not be as successful as they might be. The benefit of having access to a large number of diverse ideas is that they provide you with a future resource. Even the best of recognition ideas get old after awhile, so you need to plan for variety and rotation. Consider using one of the following ways to collect information from people in your organization about their views on recognition ideas:

- Put out a stack of cards next to a treat (edible) of some sort and ask people to help themselves to the treat in exchange for a recognition idea. (This works especially well at Halloween.)

- Collect ideas at the end of workshops—this could be an excellent closing activity for your recognition workshops.
- Use a *whip*, a simple-to-answer question that is asked of everyone in attendance at a meeting or workshop. The facilitator asks the question and then quickly polls the audience, asking each person in turn to respond. This technique is frequently used as a closing activity. For example, What is the best recognition you ever gave/got/heard about? (Fill in your own blank). This simple process of verbal sharing helps expand the recognition-giving horizons of all in attendance.
- Use your E-mail system to solicit ideas from all employees.
- Put a box (decorated and strategically located) for ideas in a common area, perhaps in the lunch room, by the coffee machine, or near a main passage way.
- Add a prize drawing to the idea submission process. From all those collected, draw out "×" number and give a gift of some sort.

SPECIFIC WAYS OF RECOGNIZING EMPLOYEE CONTRIBUTIONS

Each person in your organization does countless things during an average work week that could be recognized by other team members or by the company through its management team. Some efforts representative of the types of contributions that should be considered for recognition include the following:

Productivity and quality of work.

Innovation.

Demonstration of a behavior supporting business strategies—focus on small acts.

Attendance.

Exceptional customer service.

Risk taking and initiative.

Meeting deadlines.

Applying on the job a skill that was recently taught in a class the individual attended.

Peer support—team player.

Attitude reflecting the organization's business philosophy.

SELECTING RECOGNITION IDEAS

Consider the ideas included in this chapter as a beginning point. Add your own ideas. Be creative, and include as many people as you can in both the "dreaming-up" process and in the giving activity itself. Build in fun.

The recognition ideas in this chapter are presented in table format and are categorized to help you quickly access ideas appropriate to your particular needs at any recognition-giving moment. Ideas can be adapted to several of the listed categories—for example, food can range from simple, low-cost fare that individuals can easily afford, to team-owned with all members pitching in, to pricey meals that the senior managers or company recognition budgets assume responsibility for. You, the giver, will need to decide how to use any recognition idea, based on how you wish to personalize it to meet your particular giving opportunity.

Corporate-controlled recognition. These recognition ideas are controlled by the company. They frequently involve money (whether given directly as dollars or as nonmonetary gifts purchased by the company) and are funded by a budget. When the recognition is nonmonetary, it usually results in some type of honor bestowed by the company to specific individuals for outstanding contribution. Most corporately controlled forms of reward and recognition are built upon a fairly structured process that must be followed. These can require paperwork, and there may be limitations around who can access the program.

Peer-to-peer recognition. These ideas are targeted at individuals who want to recognize the contribution made by a fellow worker. They are designed for spontaneous giving, and the effort to prepare them is generally a manual-labor type effort rather than a dollar resource allocation. In some cases, the company must provide the basic resources that all employees can draw upon. For example, some companies designate an individual or department the task to come up with no-cost tokens such as pats-on-the-back and blue ribbons and to make sure that supplies are readily available to all interested employees.

Team-based giving. Ideas that are appropriate for team giving can cross all boundaries of the reward spectrum. They can be formal, driven by corporate regulations. They can also be of the spontaneous, low or no-cost variety. It is becoming more common for teams to be given a discretionary bonus pool with the team responsible for deciding how to allocate the dollars. Teams need to spend some time addressing exactly how they wish to deal with recognition. Individual differences will need to be accommodated. It is not uncommon for teams to adopt some particular recognition as the team's—it becomes an *insider thing* that members know about and share among themselves.

> Example: A team creates its own "trophy" for a specific be-
> havior (serious or funny) that is passed among members.
> One team had its own stuffed gorilla who was "owned" by
> the member with the greatest workload. The gorilla was
> chosen to recognize the gargantuan effort being put forth
> by its owner at that time and it served as a signal to other
> members to leave the person alone or to come by to help.

The entries in Table 7–1 are categorized by food, nonmonetary gifts and merchandise, nontangibles, personalized and handmade, and monetary. Identify those that will
work for your organization. Additional ways to think
about an idea also include:

- Low/no cost—these recognition ideas are ones that
  require more personal energy than dollars for their
  creation. They are the little tokens that one gives to a
  co-worker as a way of saying thank you. To be most
  effective they need to be timed appropriately (i.e., give
  the person the token right after she makes her
  contribution). These ideas are most commonly used as
  peer-to-peer and team recognition ideas.

- Quick preparation time—these are recognition options
  you want at hand to pull from when you see a "little"
  something you want to reinforce immediately—the
  coupon you fill out or the "gold" coin you give
  someone to reflect recognition for a small, specific act.

- Informal/requires minimal preplanning—these ideas
  are ones that individuals and teams generally have
  greater control over. No company bureaucracy is
  included. They also are ones that can be less
  personalized because personalization takes time. An
  example night be the team spontaneously taking a
  joint coffee break because the customer bought off on
  the project.

- Private/public—here the focus is on where recognition can be given. This category helps you to think about the person receiving the recognition— remember that some people are offended by public presentation while others thrive on it.
- Performance-based/presence-based—identifies what is being recognized. Some recognition, such as an award for perfect attendance for a period of time, recognizes a person's presence on the job and doesn't look at what is done during the day. Other recognition focuses on value-added contribution regardless of the time involvement. (Both types of recognition are appropriate. Just be sure you are recognizing what it is you are trying to reinforce.)

As you plan for how you will recognize others in the organization, two points to remember:

1. You can't rely on only one form of recognition—plan for diversity.
2. You can never say, "Thank you," too often to those you work with!

HOW TO USE THE MATRIX

The matrix in Table 7–1 is yours to personalize to your particular situation. Any idea can be made to fit almost any category. You need to decide how to interpret an idea based on your organization.

For example: Lunch ordered in for the team.

- This could fit in the corporate category if it was a regular event that teams could participate in by completing the required corporate paperwork in order to have lunch brought it.
- It could be a peer-to-peer option. A person simply orders lunch for a teammate who is working through lunch on a project of mutual interest.

- It could be a shared lunch that serves as a team building activity.
- The cost could range from low cost to very pricey depending on where the lunch is ordered from.
- It can be prepared quickly if lunch is a spur-of-the-moment telephone call to a local eatery.
- It will be quite informal and require minimal preplanning if it is simply eaten at the common worktable or at the workstation. However, if there is a theme with decorations, it can become more formal and take more planning.
- It can be quite private if the lunch is within the work area. It can be very public if banners are made and tables decorated.
- It can be either performance or presence based, depending on what is being recognized

Recognition is simply an act of giving that you apply to a specific setting. To help you think of recognition in different ways, the ideas in the matrix have been categorized as food, written recognition and public acknowledgment, nonmonetary gifts and merchandise, nontangibles, personalized and made, and monetary. These particular categories reflect the natural groupings of the many ideas we gathered from individuals we have queried about their recognition-giving preferences.

As an additional help, other ways of looking at the recognition idea entries have been entered across the columns.

How you apply the ideas in the matrix will depend on both your personal style and your organizational needs. Some ways you can use the matrix include the following:

- Use the list as a resource or idea list. Read through it any time you wish to recognize someone and select the idea that feels right at that moment.

- Go through the entries in the column to the left and highlight those that you can use in your organization. This will allow quick future reference when you plan to recognize someone in your organization. The highlighted matrix can be made public so that anyone looking for a way to recognize others can go to this common recognition resource list. This can be done for the organization at large or each team can have its own highlighted list to reflect the personality of the specific team.

- Select a specific column category, such as team-based, and go through the ideas in the idea column while checking off those that can be adapted to the column of interest. You can do this for more than one column, such as team-based and no or low cost, and then identify those ideas that satisfy both your criteria. Any number of criteria can be identified at one time.

- Use the matrix as a log of recognition you or your organization have given in the past. Check off ideas as you use them. This can help you establish patterns and formulate future giving plans. Your pattern should range across all columns and categories.

TABLE 7–1
Reward and Recognition Idea Matrix

Idea	Corporate Controlled	Peer-to-Peer Driven	Team-Based	Low/No Cost	
With Food					
1. Lunch ordered in for the team.					
2. A pizza or deli sandwich for the team of the honoree in his or her name.					
3. Once-a-month/quarter potluck lunch with the team/department.					
4. Organization/divisionwide breakfast or lunch.					
5. Formal lunch once a year—to be held away from the workplace.					
6. Service recognition dinner/lunch (be sure it is very nice).					
7. Lunch in someone's honor to recognize a major accomplishment.					
8. Department-sponsored lunch out for the whole team.					
9. Lunch out with the boss in a restaurant of the individual's choice.					
10. A meal with the CEO/president or top person in your organizational unit (if the team feels strongly enough about this, you might consider paying for the meal and not expect the hosting person to pay).					
11. A pizza party for the team/department.					

	Quick Preparation Time	Informal/Requires Minimal Pre-planning	Private/ Public	Performance Based/Presence-Based	Other as Appropriate to the Environment

TABLE 7–1
(continued)

Idea	Corporate Controlled	Peer-to-Peer Driven	Team-Based	Low/No Cost	
12. For one day, week, or month, free eating in the company cafeteria (this would be an individual reward).					
13. For one day per month, free eating in the company cafeteria for the entire work unit. In conjunction with this, you might consider putting up banners in the eating area to broadcast the effort being recognized.					
14. Personalized candy—a letter of the person's name or a shape that is significant, engraved chocolate (For example: A chocolate "Q" for everyone on the quality team).					
15. A dinner certificate for two with a maximum dollar amount set—this rewards the individual and the significant other.					
16. Dinner out for two for the "Employee of the Month."					
17. Lunch certificates good in a local eatery or the company cafeteria.					
18. Lunch outings for the entire group (this can even be an everyone-pays-his-own-way event. The value is in the going, so encourage but don't force anyone who isn't comfortable going with the group).					
19. "Lunch on me" coupons.					

	Quick Preparation Time	Informal/Requires Minimal Pre-planning	Private/ Public	Performance Based/Presence-Based	Other as Appropriate to the Environment

TABLE 7–1
(continued)

Idea	Corporate Controlled	Peer-to-Peer Driven	Team-Based	Low/No Cost	
20. Lifesavers are great for whimsy messages: • A necklace made up of Lifesavers rolls for being the lifesaver of _____ (fill in the blank). • A note with the message: "Thank you, you are a _____ (attach a roll of Lifesavers)."					
21. Gold chocolate coins to be given "freely."					
22. Popcorn and lemonade as a Friday afternoon snack (could be any food or drink provided on any given day).					
23. Have some candy handy, and when you notice someone doing a good job give the person a handful.					
24. Food provided for groups or individuals who are working overtime or weekends.					
25. For a small thank you, an ice cream bar or frozen yogurt.					
26. Free coffee or soft drink delivered to the person's desk (can be for one day or several).					
27. Candy, cookie, or a sweet treat, provided "just because."					
28. A week of free drinks at the cafeteria (or local coffee shop)—provide two or three per day.					

	Quick Preparation Time	Informal/Requires Minimal Pre-planning	Private/ Public	Performance Based/Presence-Based	Other as Appropriate to the Environment

TABLE 7–1
(continued)

Idea	Corporate Controlled	Peer-to-Peer Driven	Team-Based	Low/No Cost	
29. Candy bar awards within a team or department. Choose something meaningful and make it traditional: examples include a "Mr. Goodbar" award the "ABAZABA" team award.					
30. Doughnuts, bagels, rolls as an early morning starter.					
31. Buckets of candy to put out with a note of thanks—this can be to recognize a special day or for a job well done (be specific about the reason).					
32. A catered theme lunch—a hot dog wagon, Mexican fiesta, etc.					
33. Traveling? Bring back a treat indigenous to the area you visited (e.g., macadamia chocolate candies from Hawaii, pralines from New Orleans, etc.)					
34. Suckers with labels that say "Thank You."					
35. Lots of candy bars have interesting names—you can create a "story" around the thank you and attach candy with appropriate names in the right places (examples: Lifesavers, Milky Way, Hershey's Kisses, PayDay, Symphony).					

	Quick Preparation Time	Informal/Requires Minimal Pre-planning	Private/ Public	Performance Based/Presence-Based	Other as Appropriate to the Environment

TABLE 7–1
(continued)

Idea	Corporate Controlled	Peer-to-Peer Driven	Team-Based	Low/No Cost	
36. Keep some healthy food around to share or give—granola bars, fruit (fresh/dried), trail mix, pretzels. Look for treats that are low in fat.					
37. Sometimes homemade is nice—if you have a specialty, share it.					
38. Fruit/vegetables from your garden.					
39. Novelty food to recognize exceptional behavior (examples: all-day suckers, yard-long beef sticks, yard-long licorice ropes).					
40. Keep a gumball machine filled with gum, candy, or nuts and give pennies to "buy" a treat.					
41. A box of candy, nuts, or fruit.					
42. A small wooden breadboard with a deli sandwich to present to the 'hero(ine)s' of the work unit or project.					
43. A picnic, either indoors or out.					
Add your own special food favorites here:					

	Quick Preparation Time	Informal/Requires Minimal Pre-planning	Private/ Public	Performance Based/Presence-Based	Other as Appropriate to the Environment

TABLE 7–1
(continued)

Idea	Corporate Controlled	Peer-to-Peer Driven	Team-Based	Low/No Cost	
With Written Recognition and Public Acknowledgment					
1. A handwritten note of appreciation from you to your peer's family.					
2. A personal letter of thanks to the employee from the CEO/senior manager for a significant contribution (you might need to get the information to this person before the letter can be written).					
3. A personal letter of thanks to the family from the CEO/senior manager for a significant contribution (provide the information for this letter if necessary).					
4. A note/memo about the accomplishment to go into the person's personnel file—anyone can generate such a letter and move it through the company channels.					
5. Thank-you letter/memo/ note/E-mail message from anyone to anyone written in a timely manner (doing it is more important than format).					
6. Complimentary letters or memos included in a company publication or communication (have a special bulletin board in a prominent spot; circulate the letter within the department or by using E-mail; print the letter in the company newsletter or magazine).					

	Quick Preparation Time	Informal/Requires Minimal Pre-planning	Private/ Public	Performance Based/Presence-Based	Other as Appropriate to the Environment

TABLE 7–1
(continued)

Idea	Corporate Controlled	Peer-to-Peer Driven	Team-Based	Low/No Cost	
7. A posting of a person's picture, name, and why the recognition is being given (circulate a flyer; publish in the company newsletter/newspaper/magazine; post on the bulletin board).					
8. A periodical designed to recognize individuals or teams.					
9. For someone who isn't in your work unit—a thank-you letter sent to the person's boss. Be sure you are specific in giving your recognition.					
10. A thank-you letter sent to the person *at home* especially nice if it is handwritten.					
11. A special "Wall of Fame" to publicly recognize people and their accomplishments (can be individual or team-focused depending upon the company culture).					
12. A company Certificate of Achievement that is made available upon request (any individual within the company can use this to recognize the contributions of a peer—this is *not* a management tool).					
13. Employee of the month (or any other specified time frame). This could be for any level within the organization: team, department, division, or entire company.					

	Quick Preparation Time	Informal/Requires Minimal Pre-planning	Private/ Public	Performance Based/Presence-Based	Other as Appropriate to the Environment

TABLE 7–1
(continued)

Idea	Corporate Controlled	Peer-to-Peer Driven	Team-Based	Low/No Cost	
14. Team accomplishments highlighted in public—don't forget to take a team picture (circulate a flyer; publish in the company newsletter/newspaper/magazine; post it on the bulletin board).					
15. Post or give to the person a picture or caricature—let the picture tell the story of the accomplishment.					
16. A file of appropriate certificates that are readily available and that can be accessed by anyone who wishes to recognize a peer.					
17. Let the person you are recognizing know what you are doing or requesting on his or her behalf (i.e., send the person a copy of your requesting memo). Even if upper management doesn't approve the request, the person will know you were trying.					
18. A special message to say thank you or recognize an accomplishment—it can be a letter, poem, rebus, song.					
19. An "Exemplifying Excellence" or "Achievements of the Month/Quarter" bulletin board—people and their accomplishments posted (pictures, letters of commendation, descriptions of work done).					

	Quick Preparation Time	Informal/Requires Minimal Pre-planning	Private/ Public	Performance Based/Presence- Based	Other as Appropriate to the Environment

TABLE 7–1
(continued)

Idea	Corporate Controlled	Peer-to-Peer Driven	Team-Based	Low/No Cost	
20. A certificate maker PC package that will allow anyone to make an appropriate (serious or humorous) certificate or banner on the spot to recognize contributions.					
21. Acknowledge a person's contribution to a project in the cover memo accompanying the project's documentation.					
Add your own special favorites here:					
Nonmonetary with Gifts/Merchandise					
1. A paid, full membership to a professional association (can be for a year or lifetime).					
2. Paid subscription to a professional magazine or newsletter.					
3. Business cards with a card case, perhaps with the company logo on it.					

	Quick Preparation Time	Informal/Requires Minimal Pre-planning	Private/ Public	Performance Based/Presence-Based	Other as Appropriate to the Environment

TABLE 7–1
(continued)

Idea	Corporate Controlled	Peer-to-Peer Driven	Team-Based	Low/No Cost	
4. A special book associated with the person's job or personal interests, which includes pictures, letters of commendation, or job momentos. You might have key company personnel (team, peers, managers) sign it.					
5. A "funny" trophy, appropriate to the person.					
6. A "funny" trophy that is passed among team members based on "inside" criteria.					
7. A "serious" trophy appropriate to the person (this can also be one that is passed among team members based on "inside" criteria).					
8. A "tool" of the person's trade.					
9. Free car detailing or cleaning.					
10. Gift certificates or vouchers that can be used at local department stores, specialty shops, or local merchants—especially appropriate for ones that can be easily accessed during the work day.					
11. Small awards such as games, brain teasers, or puzzles.					
12. Establish criteria and then give a special pin to recognize effort or achievement (examples: taking risks, meeting quotas, etc.).					

	Quick Preparation Time	Informal/Requires Minimal Pre-planning	Private/ Public	Performance Based/Presence-Based	Other as Appropriate to the Environment

TABLE 7-1
(continued)

Idea	Corporate Controlled	Peer-to-Peer Driven	Team-Based	Low/No Cost	
13. Pins, hats, pens, T-shirts, etc. (anything with the company logo on it).					
14. Small mementos, coffee mugs, paperweights, desk paraphernalia (things that last and that are inexpensive).					
15. Small mementos to recognize completion of a big project as soon as it is over—the critical issue is your timing.					
16. Special T-shirts with a significant message tied to the project printed on the shirt. This type of recognition is very appropriate for an entire work unit. Be sure everyone knows on which day to wear their shirts—numbers can be impressive.					
17. Paper pads imprinted with the person's name, title (optional), and company logo.					
18. A supply of appropriate/ funny Post-It notes given as immediate rewards. Keep the supply visible—try using a basket or box set out in your office.					
19. Something engraved with the person's name, such as a pen set, plaque, paperweight, or cup.					

	Quick Preparation Time	Informal/Requires Minimal Pre-planning	Private/ Public	Performance Based/Presence-Based	Other as Appropriate to the Environment

TABLE 7–1
(continued)

Idea	Corporate Controlled	Peer-to-Peer Driven	Team-Based	Low/No Cost	
20. A plaque for something deemed to be best/special, given publicly. This can then be taken home and becomes an additional source of recognition.					
21. A standard recognition item (plaque/pin/loving cup) that is associated with recognition given by a particular work unit or person, or as recognition for a certain type of contribution—all will know what is being recognized and by whom when they see the item.					
22. Flowers sent to work or home.					
23. A trip to visit a significant location: the home office, some technologically appropriate learning site.					
24. Tickets to sporting events.					
25. Time away—can be for a weekend or, perhaps even better, during the week on company time. (Other department members will need to cover the job of the recognee—don't have him or her come back to an overflowing in-basket.) Ideas include: a cruise—weekend/four-day, hotel stays in nearby sites, an all-expenses-paid weekend for two.					
26. Movie tickets.					
27. Theater or concert tickets.					

	Quick Preparation Time	Informal/Requires Minimal Pre-planning	Private/ Public	Performance Based/Presence- Based	Other as Appropriate to the Environment

TABLE 7–1
(continued)

Idea	Corporate Controlled	Peer-to-Peer Driven	Team-Based	Low/No Cost	
28. Tickets to local amusement parks.					
29. One month (or more) free gym membership.					
30. A preferred parking space with or without the employee's name on it.					
31. One month (or more) free parking or transportation fees paid.					
32. Attendance at a job-related off-site: seminar, training session or workshop; professional meeting; conference. (Allow time off to attend the session and, if appropriate, the company pays the bill.)					
33. A recognition created by the peer group who decides what they will give and why it will be given.					
34. A limousine for a day.					
35. Any gift with a note of appreciation sent to the person at home. This includes the family in the recognition process.					
36. A "soap opera" break to a devotee.					

	Quick Preparation Time	Informal/Requires Minimal Pre-planning	Private/ Public	Performance Based/Presence-Based	Other as Appropriate to the Environment

TABLE 7–1

(continued)

Idea	Corporate Controlled	Peer-to-Peer Driven	Team-Based	Low/No Cost	
37. Coupon books—these provide an assortment of recognition options that the giver or receiver can select from. These can be given as books or the giver can pull out one coupon at a time. (Everyone in a department/organization might be given a book.)					
38. Tokens to accumulate and redeem.					
39. Some special support, tool, or enhancement for the individual (for example: PC upgrade, special software, new equipment).					
40. Special mementos that can be posted within the person's office (examples: a picture that is just right, a collage representing a significant project, etc.).					
41. "Behavior" coupons to reinforce a skill being emphasized by the organization or the work unit that can be quickly filled in and given on the spur of the moment to say thanks.					
42. Some type of button to recognize achievement—given to all who were involved or to special people.					
43. A significant book (professionally related or personal) and autographed with an appropriate message.					

	Quick Preparation Time	Informal/Requires Minimal Pre-planning	Private/ Public	Performance Based/Presence-Based	Other as Appropriate to the Environment

TABLE 7–1
(*continued*)

Idea	Corporate Controlled	Peer-to-Peer Driven	Team-Based	Low/No Cost	
44. Clippings of special articles on a topic you know is meaningful to the individual. Attach a note to relate the articles to something that is special to the person—an area of interest, related to earlier conversations, an area of demonstrated excellence. Demonstrates that you listened to and respected the person.					
45. Use 3 × 5 cards to write "You are special because" statements. People can collect these and reference them when things aren't going perfectly.					
46. A video of a special event or simply a montage of taped clips of everyone in the department or on the team.					
47. A product that will benefit the entire work unit, acquired on behalf of the person being recognized.					
Add your own special favorites here:					

	Quick Preparation Time	Informal/Requires Minimal Pre-planning	Private/ Public	Performance Based/Presence-Based	Other as Appropriate to the Environment
		'			

TABLE 7–1
(continued)

Idea	Corporate Controlled	Peer-to-Peer Driven	Team-Based	Low/No Cost	
Nontangibles					
1. An extra long lunch break, either immediately or in voucher form.					
2. Actively *listen* to the person, especially when the individual is discussing her accomplishment or contribution or is reacting to your recognition.					
3. Share verbal accolades. Don't forget to forward voice mail messages.					
4. Create a clear afternoon or any specified amount of uninterrupted time—a time to work alone, no meetings, time for paperwork catch-up. Remember, any time you give for this type of recognition, a teammate must cover the recognee's workload—don't make time off a punishment.					
5. Give the person the choice of the next project/assignment to work on.					
6. Build in a mechanism that allows time for brainstorming and time for research and innovation. Time is the reward. Also, if good things develop, don't forget to recognize these outputs, too.					
7. A simple, person-to-person, "Thank you for a job well done." Tell the employee *by name* that he or she is doing a good job, and be specific about what was done.					

	Quick Preparation Time	Informal/Requires Minimal Pre-planning	Private/ Public	Performance Based/Presence-Based	Other as Appropriate to the Environment

TABLE 7–1

(*continued*)

Idea	Corporate Controlled	Peer-to-Peer Driven	Team-Based	Low/No Cost	
8. Provide recognee with the opportunity to serve on a special committee.					
9. Special apparel day—jeans, tennis shoes, company T-shirt, and so on.					
10. Casual dress day—every Friday or for a set period of time: one month, one quarter, for the duration of a difficult project.					
11. Ask a person to teach or share his accomplishment with others as a way of recognizing the person's ability and role.					
12. Allow the employee to identify a specific area of job-related skill and spend a day with an in-house expert as a way of learning more about the topic.					
13. Give a recognee the opportunity to learn some aspects of a customer's business by spending a day or week with the customer.					
14. Allow time for employee group activities, such as bowling, picnics, baseball teams, and so on. (Encourage but don't force participation.)					
15. Parties!					
16. Allow a person to work at home for a day (or even half a day).					
17. Days off.					

Quick Preparation Time	Informal/Requires Minimal Pre-planning	Private/ Public	Performance Based/Presence-Based	Other as Appropriate to the Environment

TABLE 7–1
(continued)

Idea	Corporate Controlled	Peer-to-Peer Driven	Team-Based	Low/No Cost	
18. Allow the recognee to work a four-day week for a specified number of weeks.					
19. An *unexpected* afternoon off.					
20. Give a team time for an off-site and pick up any associated costs.					
21. Bring in an expert to teach a class for a team or to provide consultation.					
22. Ask a person for advice or for her opinion—this demonstrates respect.					
23. Verbally say "Thank you," or, even better, "Thank you for" . . . (specific act or contribution).					
24. A handshake.					
25. A pat on the back.					
26. A smile to acknowledge effort.					
27. Let the person report her results/outcomes to the "rest of the world."					
28. Excuse the person from an unwelcome activity.					
29. Give the person increased or changed responsibility.					
30. Give the person advance information about something upcoming that will affect his job.					

	Quick Preparation Time	Informal/Requires Minimal Pre-planning	Private/ Public	Performance Based/Presence-Based	Other as Appropriate to the Environment

TABLE 7–1

(continued)

Idea	Corporate Controlled	Peer-to-Peer Driven	Team-Based	Low/No Cost	
31. Allow the person to make a decision about things affecting his own work.					
32. Include a person in a "special" meeting.					
33. Introduce an employee to VIP's.					
34. Give social attention—"Please join me for coffee/lunch."					
35. Be sure to pass along all written compliments from customers or other management/peers—these often come in as E-mail letters or as addenda to other correspondence.					
36. Recognize an individual's accomplishments in front of peers—yours or theirs.					
37. When you hear of someone doing something special or are aware of their being commended/talked about positively by key individuals within the organization, be sure to *tell* the person. This recognition is different from formal recognition or from the person internally knowing he or she did a good job.					
38. Practice positive nonverbal behaviors that demonstrate appreciation.					

	Quick Preparation Time	Informal/Requires Minimal Pre-planning	Private/ Public	Performance Based/Presence-Based	Other as Appropriate to the Environment

TABLE 7–1
(continued)

Idea	Corporate Controlled	Peer-to-Peer Driven	Team-Based	Low/No Cost	
Add your own special favorites here:					
Personalized and Made					
1. Flowers from your garden.					
2. Building blocks as recognition of excellence or doing a good job. Can be part of a set that is given over time and that will ultimately spell something (might even be the organization/person's name).					
3. A homemade funny trophy that is appropriate to what is being recognized.					
4. A message written on any appropriate object (e.g., "You're a good apple" written on an apple ornament).					
5. A blue ribbon to recognize a contribution.					
6. Post something significant outside an individual's work space to recognize a contribution (must be understood by the work unit; can be something that is rotated among the group). Humor is most appropriate.					

	Quick Preparation Time	Informal/Requires Minimal Pre-planning	Private/ Public	Performance Based/Presence-Based	Other as Appropriate to the Environment

TABLE 7–1
(continued)

Idea	Corporate Controlled	Peer-to-Peer Driven	Team-Based	Low/No Cost	
7. A framed memento/letter/certificate.					
8. Your own special button award to be given just within your own work unit.					
9. At the beginning of the year, start a "visible something" for each person or work unit that can be added to for each accomplishment throughout the year. An example might be a poster or certificate that has space for each person's recognition tokens to be added. The key is accumulation during the year so that all can see progress.					
10. A small notepad with a significant message (many companies have printing facilities that can design, print, and bind pads, so you can be creative) to present with a pen or pencil. Example: A notepad in the shape of a telephone to recognize excellent phone service.					
11. An appropriate poem/poster/card to frame and give as recognition.					
12. A survival kit that includes things appropriate to what is being recognized (e.g., food and coffee change for people who stay late, presentation supplies for facilitators).					

	Quick Preparation Time	Informal/Requires Minimal Pre-planning	Private/ Public	Performance Based/Presence-Based	Other as Appropriate to the Environment

TABLE 7–1
(continued)

Idea	Corporate Controlled	Peer-to-Peer Driven	Team-Based	Low/No Cost	
13. Something that matches the person or action being recognized. For example: a "Gumby" key ring for being flexible, or a PayDay candy bar to someone in the payroll department.					
14. A shiny new penny for a special thought that has been shared.					
15. A box of thank you notes (whimsy or formal) kept in your desk so that you can immediately write a personal note to recognize a contribution. Nothing says thank you more than a personal note, especially when it is given in a timely manner.					
16. A plant—to reference how growth has occurred.					
17. Balloons decorated with appropriate messages.					
18. A mug filled with "treats."					
19. A "spoonful of kisses" (a plastic spoon with a few Hershey's kisses on it wrapped in cellophane and ribbon).					
20. A clear plastic clipboard personalized with the individual's name and a message identifying the accomplishment.					
21. A rope or fancy ribbon tied up in knots given to a person who straightened you out about "corporate ropes."					

	Quick Preparation Time	Informal/Requires Minimal Pre-planning	Private/ Public	Performance Based/Presence- Based	Other as Appropriate to the Environment

TABLE 7–1
(continued)

Idea	Corporate Controlled	Peer-to-Peer Driven	Team-Based	Low/No Cost	
22. An assortment of stickers to place onto documents to recognize and reinforce a job well done.					
23. A ruler given to a person who set you straight about rules and regulations.					
24. A set of recognition masters that can be easily duplicated onto colorful stock and completed and used by everyone in the organizational unit. When these are quick and easy to use, they encourage immediate peer recognition of effort.					
25. Pens or pencils embossed with an appropriate message.					
26. 3-D geometric shapes or origami-like objects that can be written on—thank-you messages can be personalized and the object is a work-of-art.					
27. Create a mobius with a special, continuous message of appreciation.					
28. A banner strung across the work area to publicize a contribution or accomplishment (can be for an individual or for a group).					
29. A desk toy: stress balls, a nerf basketball set, and so on.					

	Quick Preparation Time	Informal/Requires Minimal Pre-planning	Private/ Public	Performance Based/Presence- Based	Other as Appropriate to the Environment

TABLE 7–1
(continued)

Idea	Corporate Controlled	Peer-to-Peer Driven	Team-Based	Low/No Cost	
30. Your own personal something to give others to let them know you appreciate their effort—could range from some type of candy you always leave, to a meaningful sticker, to a single flower. Whatever you choose will become your personal trademark of thanks.					
31. A posted project/task chart to recognize group progress toward a common goal—be sure this reflects *group* process and doesn't single out individuals.					
32. A large calendar that can be posted. Call it the celebration calendar and use Post-Its and written notes of recognition tacked onto specific dates to honor contributions made by team members.					
33. Magnets with appropriate messages or designs—these are quick and easy items to give. One can be significant or individuals can collect many to reflect their contributions.					
Add your own special favorites here:					

	Quick Preparation Time	Informal/Requires Minimal Pre-planning	Private/ Public	Performance Based/Presence-Based	Other as Appropriate to the Environment

TABLE 7–1
(continued)

Idea	Corporate Controlled	Peer-to-Peer Driven	Team-Based	Low/No Cost	
*Monetary**					
1. Dollars for suggestions.					
2. Senior manager walks the area, giving $5.00 (any dollar amount could be used) to anyone who demonstrates whatever the organization is emphasizing. Generally this would be part of a plan to supports strategic business goals.					
3. Two-dollar bills as a reward for whatever is deemed rewardable. Everyone could be given bills to distribute or it could be done by managers.					
4. An incentive-like program—an individual/manager sets a goal outside the usual work responsibilities to be rewarded with a predetermined or negotiated amount.					
5. Spot bonuses.					
6. Bonuses given at a group level—the group must earn and share.					
.. A bonus for anyone who comes up with and implements an idea that saves dollars—a percentage of the dollars saved is given as a bonus.					
8. Travelers/negotiable checks.					

	Quick Preparation Time	Informal/Requires Minimal Pre-planning	Private/ Public	Performance Based/Presence-Based	Other as Appropriate to the Environment

TABLE 7–1
(concluded)

Idea	Corporate Controlled	Peer-to-Peer Driven	Team-Based	Low/No Cost	
Add your own special favorites here:					

*Generally, monetary recognition must be driven by management. It is important to remember that giving monetary recognition opens a whole different set of considerations because of taxation issues. For this reason, the entire area of formalized bonus programs has purposefully been omitted from this book. If you are looking for a simple monetary recognition, you might consider the items listed in this section—they were repeatedly mentioned by the various groups queried in gathering the material for this book.

	Quick Preparation Time	Informal/Requires Minimal Pre-planning	Private/ Public	Performance Based/Presence- Based	Other as Appropriate to the Environment
		·			

Index

Other books of interest to you from Irwin Professional Publishing include the following:

UNLEASHING PRODUCTIVITY!
Your Guide to Unlocking the Secrets of Super Performance

Richard Ott with Martin Snead

This quick read to becoming more creative, productive, and satisfied shows how to recognize and remove productivity barriers. Packed with tips, techniques, and ideas that show how to get the most from your workforce and yourself. (200 pages)
1–55623–931–9

FROM VISION TO BEYOND TEAMWORK
10 Ways to Wake Up and Shake Up Your Company

Nicola Phillips and Trish Denoon

Sums up the most innovative management techniques from around the world, with special emphasis on where the ideas come from and how they are used. (250 pages)
0–7863–0318–2

MOTIVATION AT WORK

Business Skills Express Series

Jane R. Miskell and Vincent Miskell

Filled with creative approaches to behavior modification and
management, this guide shows supervisors and managers how to
identify and conquer the problems that can keep employees from
performing at peak levels. Offers suggestions for handling all types of
unmotivated employees. (100 pages)
1–55623–868–1